Seeking Balance

The Story of a Principal's Second Semester

Nicholas J. Pace

ROWMAN & LITTLEFIELD EDUCATION
A division of
ROWMAN & LITTLEFIELD
Lanham • Boulder • New York • Toronto • Plymouth, UK

Published by Rowman & Littlefield Education
A division of Rowman & Littlefield
4501 Forbes Boulevard, Suite 200, Lanham, Maryland 20706
www.rowman.com

10 Thornbury Road, Plymouth PL6 7PP, United Kingdom

Copyright © 2014 Nicholas J. Pace

All rights reserved. No part of this book may be reproduced in any form or by any electronic or mechanical means, including information storage and retrieval systems, without written permission from the publisher, except by a reviewer who may quote passages in a review.

British Library Cataloguing in Publication Information Available

Library of Congress Cataloging-in-Publication Data

Pace, Nicholas J.
Seeking balance : the story of a principal's second semester / Nicholas J. Pace.
p. cm.
Includes bibliographical references.
ISBN 978-1-4758-0669-4 (cloth : alk. paper) -- ISBN 978-1-4758-0671-7 (pbk. : alk. paper) -- ISBN 978-1-4758-0672-4 (electronic)
1. First year school principals--United States--Case studies. 2. High school principals--United States--Case studies. 3. School year--United States--Case studies. I. Title.
LB2831.92.P353 2013
371.2'012--dc23
2013042247

♾️™ The paper used in this publication meets the minimum requirements of American National Standard for Information Sciences Permanence of Paper for Printed Library Materials, ANSI/NISO Z39.48-1992.

Printed in the United States of America

For my parents. No two ever did more.

Contents

Acknowledgments		vii
Preface		ix
Introduction		1
1	Early January: The Second Half	3
2	Late January: Reaching Out	19
3	Early February: Politics, Authenticity, and Support	35
4	Late February: Data, Evidence, and Unpredictability	49
5	March: Capacity, Silence, Tension, and Tears	69
6	Early April: Creativity	85
7	Late April: Never Saw That Coming	105
8	May: Cupcakes, Boundaries, and the Paradox	121
References		139

Acknowledgments

As with this book's predecessor and companion, *Reality Calling: The Story of a Principal's First Semester*, I owe many people my heartfelt thanks. Tom Koerner, Caitlin Crawford, and Laura Reiter of Rowman & Littlefield Education are an author's dream in terms of vision, professionalism, and support.

As explained in *Reality Calling*, many school administrators, attorneys, psychologists, and parents helped inspire the stories in both books. They are too numerous to thank but know who they are. Likewise, Jeff Dieken, Troyce Fisher, Steve Foster, Betty Hogan, and Dewitt Jones, along with students enrolled in the 2012 All-Iowa Principalship Cohort at the University of Northern Iowa, shared valuable insights on a painfully rough initial draft of this project in the fall of 2012. My friend and mentor John K. Smith was, as always, direct, pragmatic, creative, and generous. Kathy Collins Reilly was her magnificent self. Finally, Roxanne, Sienna, and Adison Pace did what they always do.

Preface

Charts, test scores, trend lines, and percentages, while useful and important, can never capture the full essence of what it means to be a principal, but stories have a chance. This book's companion and predecessor, *Reality Calling: The Story of a Principal's First Semester*, was my first effort to illuminate the life of a principal through fiction. *Seeking Balance: The Story of a Principal's Second Semester* reveals the rest of that story and was driven by the same goals.

First, it seeks to remind readers that nothing is out of the realm of possibility in terms of what principals might encounter on a given day. The heartbreaking, heartwarming, and heart-pounding stories principals share with me daily remind me of that fact. Second, I hope to caution new principals about the danger of thinking they have or *should have* all the answers. A good many of the challenges principals face are simply too big to tackle alone. Finally, both books seek to portray principals not as mindless cogs in a massive, faceless machine or as infallible super heroes, but as real people, toiling every day to be real-world difference makers.

Seeking Balance completes the story that began in *Reality Calling*. Taken together, I invite readers to formulate authentic, standards-based, practical judgments about the degree to which Principal Joe Gentry and his two friends (also new principals) meet the challenges of school leadership in their first year.

Introduction

Seeking Balance picks up where *Reality Calling* left off. Principal Joe Gentry and his two grad school friends have navigated their first semesters as principals. In December, they met at a familiar campus hangout to reflect upon the realities of school leadership, lessons learned, and their successes and setbacks. With renewed energy and a few months of real-world experience, they draw a collective breath and step into the second half of the school year.

Seeking Balance begins in January with Joe's much anticipated midyear evaluation with the associate superintendent and moves into myriad issues—some evolving from decisions and events that took place in the first semester in *Reality Calling*, while others appear at a moment's notice from out of the blue. As must all principals, Joe seeks to strike the right balance between leadership and management, personal and professional life, pushing and pulling, speaking and listening.

As winter turns to spring, Joe and his grad school friends work to apply lessons learned, improve themselves and their schools, and navigate the ever-present complicated and competing interests of the principalship. The story concludes in May when Joe anticipates his end-of-the-year evaluation, looks to the future, and reflects upon the Paradox of the Principalship.

Chapter One

Early January

The Second Half

Joe's winter break meeting with his grad school friends-turned-new-principals Kristi and Sutt was perfectly timed and a much-needed vacation. Although it initially seemed that getting together would be too difficult, they made it happen after Joe's mentor, Pinicon Elementary Principal Tom McHale, insisted. The gathering allowed them to think about their first semester successes, shortcomings, and goals for the second half of the school year. It also reinforced the importance of getting away from school, both mentally and physically.

Joe found the latter easier than the former. He, his wife, Claire, four-year-old Margaret, and fifteen-year-old Elliott spent a few days seeing family but made establishing their own family traditions in Pinicon a priority. In between holiday gatherings, his thoughts returned to Pinicon Secondary.

Joe liked the way Kessler and Pinicon's shared superintendent Dr. Carol Zylstra always began administrative meetings by asking "What's new and good?" and then gave each principal an opportunity to answer. He hoped Associate Superintendent Don Mitchell's evaluation would include Joe's goals for the second half of the year. In the new year's edition of his blog, Joe shared the practice and how important he felt it was to have a sense of renewal. He wrote that he hoped Pinicon teachers were coming back refreshed and that he was excited for the leadership team to share two new opportunities.

Back in October, Joe had convinced Zylstra to allow Pinicon the freedom to choose how to spend some professional learning money, rather than automatically following Kessler's plan. When she agreed, Joe passed the opportunity on to the leadership team with the caveat that whatever the direction taken, it needed to connect to the ongoing effort to define the Pinicon Way.

He was encouraged when the team's focus was on teachers sharing and collaborating. As a result, he and Cal Murphy, principal at Kessler High, put the two leadership teams in contact to explore a new program called TeachShare, which combined electronic real-time communication and sharing via distance and a long list of prompts for discussion and relationship building. Teachers in both schools and a nationwide network of others could sign up for common interest groups related to methods, particular challenges, student ages, or curricular areas of interest. He and Murphy were especially pleased with teachers' responses and were excited that the electronic interactions between teachers could be strengthened by face-to-face collaboration since Pinicon and Kessler were so close.

The program also allowed Joe to engage with administrators at Kessler and elsewhere around school leadership. This allowed him to honestly tell his staff that he would be learning along with them using the same tool. He didn't share that it also allowed him to invisibly observe teachers' engagement and use of the system, though he doubted he would use the feature. *Too Big Brother-ish*, he thought.

The second new and good item was the hiring of Heidi Morris as an on-demand floating substitute teacher. She had taught for a few years and earned a master's degree in curriculum before leaving education to join her husband in pharmaceutical sales. She quickly soured on sales, however, and began substitute teaching, making it known that she hoped to return to teaching. The floating sub position would allow teachers to spend time observing each other's classrooms and collaborating. Although not all teachers felt they were "ready," Joe said interest was strong enough to justify the cost, which was covered by school sharing money from the state.

Joe knew Associate Superintendent Don Mitchell might not see the value in the idea, so he first pitched it to Zylstra, tying the argument to the TeachShare program and pointing out that there was state money to support these efforts for sharing districts like Pinicon and Kessler. Armed with Zylstra's blessing, Joe made sure Mitchell knew she was on board when he shared his plan. He had learned that Mitchell's first answer when it came to spending money was usually no, even if there were funds available. He had also observed that while Mitchell was often standoffish and gruff, he rarely challenged Zylstra. Joe smiled, anxious to share the way he was working district politics with Professor Summers.

The benefits to hiring the energetic Heidi Morris were hard to count. The flexible, floating sub position allowed her to get back into education while still enjoying her newborn daughter and the massive new house she and her husband had built overlooking the Pinicon River. And her teaching experience, master's in curriculum, and credibility were welcomed by the staff. *A key step forward*, Joe thought.

A COLD WIND AND CLARITY

Joe had also experienced an unexpected moment of clarity during the winter break. It involved his interaction with Merle Richards—another topic he suspected Mitchell would bring up. It struck him one cold day while running that the way he had engaged Richards was inconsistent with what attracted him to the principalship and had been all wrong. He reflected about a speaker from grad school who implored principals to be sparks for others' success.

He revisited the intensity and shock everyone felt after the shop accident the previous fall and extensive time spent on safety and adherence to the plan that had been developed. Realizing that Richards had been doing it basically alone smacked him like the January wind. He shared his insight with Kristi on the phone.

"I've totally mishandled Richards," he said.

"What do you mean?" Kristi asked.

"I've gone at this all wrong. Remember that speaker from the administrator's association talking about principals as the *spark for success*? I've been anything but that. Professor Summers taught us that providing support and creating conditions for success is *our job*, right?"

She agreed.

"Well, the fact is, I haven't done that. Richards shared his concerns about behavior and class size and I basically ignored them. I looked it up and his average class size has been twenty something. My gut said that was a lot for the space he's got, yet I did nothing with it last fall. Throw in some rowdy kids, well . . . that's a tough haul. And he's been going it alone, at least since I've been here. He's had a scowling principal, but no support."

"So, you've changed your opinion about him?"

"The accident clouded my vision. I bitched about the whole situation being a headache. Now I realize the headache was because *my approach was all wrong*. I made it *about me* rather than supporting teachers and kids. He's not a bad guy or teacher. Knows his stuff, but he's got a small space, some tough kids, and a principal that's done nothing to help. *Zero.* It took me four months to see that I was falling into the role of a throwback principal, not matching up with what we were taught. Feels like I was *becoming Don Mitchell*. Ugh."

Thus, another of Joe's goals was to restart his efforts with Richards in a more productive direction. That involved asking Richards to meet him at the shop the day before classes resumed. The teacher seemed apprehensive and cautiously asked Joe if there was something he needed.

"Just a conversation and a coffee partner," Joe said. "I'm just gonna say it. Merle, I know you're working hard at this. I realized over break that you've been working at it *alone*, and that's not what I pledged to do when I got into this. That isolation is on me and I want to change it."

Richards studied him quizzically. "What are you getting at?"

"That accident last fall scared everybody and I've been hawking over you like a guard. I don't want to do that. I want to be involved in helping teachers succeed. I've looked back at the materials you gave me last fall about class size. Last week I went in and capped your classes at fourteen students. You shared that concern with me last fall and I should've done it then. It's too crowded down here for numbers pushing twenty plus."

Richards looked taken aback. "Well, thank you for that. What are you asking me to do?"

Joe paused. "To trust that I want to help. I wonder if we could start by meeting early a couple of mornings a week to talk about stuff. Your plans, curriculum, the kids, ideas, that sort of thing. I'd like to offer support and be a partner rather than an enforcer," Joe said.

"Or a spy?" Richards said dryly.

Joe sighed. "Think about it. Tuesday about 7:15? I'll bring the donuts. Let me know," Joe said as he headed out. It felt good to make the offer and extend the hand, but he didn't know how Richards would respond. *Trust takes time and I'm getting a late start.*

ANTICIPATION

In addition to his goals for the semester, Joe had spent a lot of time anticipating his midyear evaluation with Associate Superintendent Mitchell, which was inconveniently scheduled for the first day back from break. Joe was glad Kristi had injected some professional conversation into their holiday gathering at the Northgate Grill; otherwise, they might have just swapped stories about bizarre events from their first few months on the job. He knew that Mitchell was chiefly focused on the management aspects of being principal, particularly paperwork and student discipline.

Joe's venerable favorite professor, Darrell Summers, had insisted that principals couldn't earn the license to lead instruction until they had demonstrated they could handle day-to-day management. While not perfect and certainly not without his critics, Joe felt reasonably competent as a manager.

Failing to crack the (minor in his mind) case of homecoming vandalism and the theft of $3,500 from the Pirate Invitational Wrestling Tournament in December led Joe to wonder if Mitchell would be dinging him in this area while overlooking his efforts to be highly visible in classrooms and establish a new focus on instruction, not to mention his overarching goal of collaboratively defining the Pinicon Way. Sitting outside Mitchell's office waiting to discuss the midyear evaluation, he wondered if Claire was right—that Joe was his own toughest critic.

HOW'D IT GO, JOE?

Predictably, Joe's phone chirped almost as soon as his meeting with Mitchell ended.

"How'd it go, Joe?" Sutt asked.

"It was kind of weird. I was expecting this formal thing based on the way Mitchell had talked about it. We started about 40 minutes late and just talked. Nothing formal at all."

"Why did he keep you waiting so long?"

"Dunno. Said some new year stuff had come up, but I was a little frustrated. I lost a couple hours, and you know how I hate being out of the building," Joe said.

When Sutt pressed for more specifics, Joe said Mitchell had stressed the importance of management and its connection to the principal being seen as credible. As Joe expected, Mitchell mentioned the homecoming vandalism and money theft from the wrestling tournament, describing them as "important but not unusual setbacks."

"I said I agree that management has to be in order for anything good to happen. But I think we differ on how important the homecoming stuff and missing money are. I've moved on and am not willing to give that a ton of time. Even the police couldn't solve them," Joe said. "Claire says I shouldn't discount what Mitchell says just because I don't think he's much of a leader. I know I can learn from him, and I sure as hell don't want to alienate him or seem uninterested. It's just frustrating that he doesn't seem more interested in bigger-picture stuff."

"Your wife is smart."

"She is. I'm really excited about some teaching and learning stuff that's coming up, but he didn't ask about that, my goals for the rest of the year, or what I've learned. I just think we have different visions of leadership."

"That's probably not all bad. You know what matters to him, so go do it and then push ahead on your own stuff," Sutt suggested.

EMPOWERING EDUCATORS

Joe looked over the applications for the Empowering Educators Conference and smiled. All of the names he had hoped to see were there. Carole Martinson, Allison Jesup, Mark Watters, and Rhonda Prior had completed applications. Kessler High Principal Cal Murphy also had an enthusiastic group of teachers who were ready to go. Many were members of their building's leadership team. Joe and Murphy hoped their teachers' attendance would jump-start use of the TeachShare program between the schools.

"We've got two more spots. I think Gregg Altman should go, which is a two-for-one, since he's shared between our buildings. Since I didn't get you a Christmas present, I'll let you fill the last spot," Murphy joked.

"I'm fine with Altman. I'd like to put Heidi Morris in there, too."

Even though she was brand new, Joe wanted Morris to attend since she would be spending so much time in covering for teachers who were collaborating. Although she was *just* a substitute, the sample lesson from her interview and teaching videos in her portfolio led Joe to conclude she was already one of the best teachers at Pinicon. He hoped to hire her into a full-time position when one became available.

Joe had not met many teachers like Altman. He was a rarity: certified to teach everything from special education, to drivers ed, health, and economics. On top of that, he liked to coach and had a knack for computers. Joe wondered if some were threatened by his acumen. Besides his multiple certifications and knack for connecting with kids, Joe liked his curious, creative nature, and he never seemed to tire.

While some teachers wanted several periods of the same course in a row, Altman thrived on some early morning driver's education, followed by a health class, facilitating some independent-study computer work, a couple of study halls, and an AP econ course, before hustling to Kessler for a health class, then back to Pinicon to coach. "I'm not great, but adequate at a lot of things," Altman liked to say. And the kids loved him.

Joe was sure the Pinicon teachers set to attend the Empowering Educators Conference were the right ones. If the conference matched its reputation, it would be time and money well spent. The principals and teachers Joe followed on Twitter said it was one of the best learning experiences they'd had. Even if the conference was marginal, the sharing between Pinicon and Kessler teachers would be a tangible benefit of the sharing agreement between the districts. *Why hadn't The Pinicon Herald covered that last fall*, he mused.

TALK US THROUGH

Zylstra had prepped Joe for his presentation to the Pinicon Board of Education. Although he had presented to them several times, this would be different. The board wanted background information on the decision to implement the Saturday School program for detention students. And since $3,500 had come up missing while Saturday School students were working at the Pirate Invitational Wrestling Tournament, the two issues had become linked in some board members' minds.

Joe decided to separate the issues in his presentation to the board. He began by sharing the same three year's worth of discipline data that he had presented to the leadership team in the fall semester. "As a team, we were looking to strengthen our discipline procedures. First, we obviously wanted to change students' behavior. Impacting their social time is often an effective way to do that. Second, we wanted to provide an opportunity for them to do something productive and perhaps help the school if they're not working on homework. Like restitution. There are a number of ways they can be of service during Saturday School."

He answered a few questions about parent reactions, how Saturday School was supervised, and whether it had improved student discipline.

"I can't give you a number. It's far too early for that, but I can say our teachers feel a tangible difference. Of course no student *wants* to be there and we don't want them to *like it*, but when there have been opportunities to actually help the school, such as at the Pirate Invitational, several students have said it felt good.

One longtime board member questioned the wisdom of beginning something in the middle of the year. "I wonder if, in hindsight, you should have thought about this a little more and started it next year."

Joe nodded. "We've worked pretty hard on team decision making. I felt we had a problem with student detentions being a meaningless waste of time and that we needed an alternative. The leadership team settled on Saturday School, which I enthusiastically supported. My feeling was—*and is*—that it's better to make the change immediately rather than go through another year of a procedure that wasn't meeting our needs."

The board member nodded politely but suggested that the theft of $3,500 from the wrestling tournament might not have happened if Saturday School had been more thoroughly thought out or more effectively implemented. After a couple other board members weighed in, Joe spoke up.

"In my mind, these are two separate issues. The Saturday School students were supervised by one of our best veteran teachers, Larry Den Herder, and our excellent AD, Frank Young, ran the tournament as he has for several years. The Pinicon police haven't been able to crack the case and have found no evidence that Saturday School kids were involved. I wish we knew who took the money, but the fact is it could have been anybody. Who knows? A fan, a student, someone in the concession area. But we're not thinking about doing away with *the tournament*. Likewise, I'd be against doing away with Saturday School."

Board member Gene DeVore nodded and Don Mitchell spoke next. "Mr. Gentry makes a good point. We wish we knew what happened, but we don't. And the wrestling tournament isn't going anywhere. If the leadership team down at Pinicon thinks Saturday School is a good idea, I think that's up to them."

Zylstra followed with praise for how Joe had used evidence to examine a problem and then looked for solutions by engaging the leadership team. "I support that," she said. "While the theft is unfortunate, there's no way we can conclude it has anything to do with Saturday School. As the police said, there are several hundred potential suspects. It's frustrating, but that's the reality."

That seemed to satisfy the board, which moved on to other agenda items. Joe found himself actually enjoying the rest of the meeting, particularly Cal Murphy's overview of the TeachShare initiative between their two schools and the engagement they hoped it would encourage. Chatting with a few administrators and board members after the meeting, Joe was surprised by the praise Mitchell heaped on him.

"That guy is hard to figure out," Joe whispered to Murphy.

"You're right about that. Just smile and take it," Murphy said, "because you never know what he'll do next."

THE FISHBOWL

Prior to the start of school in August, Joe and Claire had braced themselves for the amount of event supervision that came with the principalship. When he interviewed, Joe said he understood the demands on principals' time but that he and his family attended most school events anyway, so it wouldn't be much different. And for the most part, that had proven to be true.

What Joe and Claire had not fully appreciated, however, was how merely *attending* versus *attending as an administrator* was different. "I see what you mean when you talk about always being *on*," she said. "You're not just sitting there as principal. It's different being in charge of the event. I catch myself thinking about things like what I'm going to wear and who I'm talking to because people are watching. It really *is* different. And I'm just the spouse."

Claire had once heard a principal's husband caution against assuming that family time and event supervision could be double-dipped by attending school events. He estimated that 85% of his outings with his wife were school related. Similarly, Claire began the new year's calendar year by highlighting dates on the calendar when no Pinicon events were scheduled. She intended to use these for date nights or family time. Even if it was just a trip to Home Depot or the grocery store, it would be some time together away from Pinicon Secondary.

In reality, the plan was less successful than Claire hoped. Even in the first few days of the month, Joe was too tired or preoccupied to make the errands feel meaningful, and having him along seemed like more work for both of them. And, winter sports were in full swing.

BAUER POWER

After the race-based harassment some of the basketball players had experienced at Piedmont High School, Joe told Young that one of them should be present at away basketball games. Like Joe, AD Frank Young wasn't looking for more nighttime activities, but agreed. Joe drew the first event—the boy-girl varsity doubleheader basketball game at Sherwood High. Despite their discussion of combining family time with event supervision, Joe suggested that he, Claire, and Margaret make it a family outing. The night turned out more pleasant than expected.

They got out of town in time to run a couple errands and grab dinner at Margaret's favorite spot—Subway. She bounced around through both games, adorable in her Pinicon Pirate cheerleader outfit, and Elliott got to play a few minutes of the varsity game—something unusual for a freshman.

The best moment by far, however, came with about two minutes to play. With the Pinicon boys comfortably ahead, the Sherwood coach was emptying his bench, allowing everyone a chance to play. One such player was an awkward, rail-thin student. As he checked into the game, the Sherwood student section began to chant, "Bauer Power, Bauer Power."

Joe was briefly uncomfortable, remembering again Professor Summers's admonition that nothing good ever happens in the stands. *Are the Sherwood kids mocking one of their classmates? How are our Pinicon kids going to respond? The Bauer kid might look even more awkward.* Joe watched as the Pinicon players huddled and the Sherwood crowd continued its chant.

After the Sherwood players passed the ball from side to side several times, the gangly Tommy Bauer ran off a screen and threw up a long jump shot that nearly went in. The crowd exhaled a collective sigh of disappointment. Pinicon took the rebound to the other end and scored quickly, returning the ball to Sherwood. The Sherwood coach held up three fingers to his team. Three of his players cut across the court and found Tommy Bauer coming across the floor in the opposite direction.

One by one, the Pinicon defenders allowed themselves to get caught up in the three screens being set for Tommy Bauer. After the third, Tommy caught a pass, set his feet and launched a slightly awkward three pointer that touched nothing but the net. The Sherwood crowd erupted, as did a good portion of the Pinicon side. Tommy Bauer grinned widely and pumped his fist. His teammates on the Sherwood bench waved towels in the air as the announcer roared, "Three pointer by Tommmmmyyyy Baaaauuuuuueerrrrrr!" Although Pinicon won the game by 18 points, the Sherwood players carried Tommy Bauer off the floor, still pumping his fist and grinning broadly.

After the game, Joe learned from a Sherwood parent that Tommy Bauer had come out for the basketball team only after being declared cancer-free following a long battle with myriad health problems. "Everybody loves that kid. I'm sure it's the first basket he's ever scored and maybe the first real game he's played in," the parent said.

Joe caught Coach Lang outside the Pinicon locker room. Lang said letting Bauer score was all the players' doing. "Maybe you saw the guys huddling to talk about it late in the game," he said. "Sam Shottenkirk is friends with the Bauer kid on Facebook. He huddled our guys and said, 'Don't make it obvious, but let that kid score.'"

"That's awesome. Do you mind if I talk to the team for thirty seconds?" Joe asked.

"Have at them," Lang offered.

In the locker room, Joe told the team what he had learned about Tommy Bauer. "I want you to know that you made a helluva memory for a young man tonight. For the entire school, really. We talk a lot about heart in sports. You guys showed a lot of heart tonight in the way you played, but more importantly what you did for Tommy Bauer. Your teachers and I have talked a lot about what *the Pinicon Way* means. I love what I saw tonight. I'm proud of you and it made my night. Thanks for that. Sam, that's some real leadership."

He would have spoken to the parents of any student involved in such a nice gesture. That it was Sam Shottenkirk gave him a chance to engage Susan on a more positive topic. *Maybe she'll see that I really don't hate the whole family*, Joe thought.

WHAT'S THAT SOUND?

Joe was touring the building with a math consultant from the state department of education who had once worked with Stu Petersen and asked to see him. As they made their way toward the gym, Joe heard strange popping and thudding sounds but tried to stay focused on the conversation with the consultant. As they entered the gym, Joe's eyes flew open wide. One group of students was using a makeshift slingshot to hurl medicine balls toward the basketball hoops. He cringed as the balls crashed off the glass backboards with what appeared to be enough force to shatter them. Next, he saw students gathered around Daniel Henshaw, who stood on the free-throw line beside a portable air-compressor with a long hose attached. Taped to the wall pad underneath the basketball hoop was a picture of a bare-chested woman sprawled across the hood of a race car. Henshaw and a group of students howled loudly as he shot finishing nails out of the hose and into the pad and picture.

"Look at that! I got her right in the . . ."

Joe couldn't believe his eyes. *Why the hell did I bring the math consultant through here?* he asked himself. "Henshaw!" Joe roared. "What are you doing?"

"It's free day, Mr. Gentry!" a student answered.

Henshaw dropped the hose, and the students around him searched desperately for a way to slide away. "What are the rest of you guys doing? Where's Mr. Petersen?" Just then, Petersen strolled in, clicking off his cell phone and said, "What's all the noise in here?"

Joe grabbed a handful of nails from the floor and pulled the poster off the wall pad. "Daniel, my office. Now. The rest of you get this place cleaned up." Petersen squinted at Joe, the poster, air hose, slingshots, and medicine balls as if he had not yet processed what had been happening. As Joe walked past him, he dropped the nails into Petersen's open palm and heard them fall to the floor. Petersen's former colleague, the math consultant, followed awkwardly behind in the now silent gym.

After the math consultant left, Joe typed out an e-mail to Petersen, asking him to meet with him the next morning, at which time he would inform him that he would be placing a formal letter of reprimand in his file. He wondered how Petersen would react.

Joe was grateful for the support Henshaw's father, Wes, offered when Joe informed him of his son's three-day suspension. "The boy needs a boot in his ass and Stu Petersen don't have the sense to do it. But I do. He'll be glad to get back to school when I'm done with him," Wes growled.

Normally, Joe preferred to suspend students in school so he could isolate them and monitor their work. He leaned away from out-of-school suspensions because they resembled vacation days for some. For others, he preferred suspending students in school because he feared how some parents might discipline their kids. But Joe liked Wes Henshaw and had a feeling that Daniel doing some hard work for a surly and embarrassed dad would be a good thing.

As was his standard practice, he told Wes that the three of them would have to meet in Joe's office on the morning after Daniel's suspension for "reentry" into school. Joe was unsure whether these meetings caused students to show any remorse for their actions. He was certain, however, that they were inconvenient for parents, which he didn't mind. On a few key occasions, he had taken Cal Murphy's advice and delayed students' reentry to their regular schedule until parents could meet.

NOT APPROPRIATE

Joe was happy with the way the leadership team was running. Although teacher leadership was a new experience for Pinicon staff, they had embraced the opportunity. Joe felt he was making good on his promise to involve them as much as possible in decisions that impacted teaching and learning in the building. Hiring Heidi Morris and sending a group to the Empowering Educators Conference had reinforced that. The team and most of the faculty seemed grateful for the attention to instruction and Joe's convincing Zylstra to allow teachers a choice in professional learning.

After student Robin Stiles stabbed herself with the pencil in Joe's office in November, he had continued with the plan to have her escorted at all times during the day. Joe took a couple of turns, along with his secretary Carrie and a couple of associates. He knew some teachers didn't see the plan as appropriate, but Joe insisted it was the best they could do, given Robin's complicated circumstances and the fact that Jeralyn, the counselor, had not returned to work following her surgery.

The leadership team meeting was wrapping up when Mark Watters spoke up. "Joe, we'd like to talk about the Robin Stiles thing."

Joe had arranged a quiet place in the nurse's office for her to use anytime she felt overwhelmed. That kept her where she could be seen and also eased some of the burden for the escorts, who were often pulled in other directions. Joe also knew that this seemed like a holding tank or special treatment to many teachers.

"There's a concern that she is exploiting the situation," Watters said. "I don't see it that way, but some teachers and kids do. She gets all this special treatment and a nice place to hang out in the office because we don't know what else to do with her."

"I didn't realize folks saw the office as such a desirable spot," Joe joked and said Robin's case was a complicated one. "It's a tough situation. Jeralyn is still out from surgery and she and Robin don't connect well. I've asked the Kessler school social worker and county mental health folks, but her parents are reluctant to give permission."

"Can't we just get her referred to special ed?" Rhonda Prior asked.

"An eval makes sense to me, Rhonda, but until her parents agree, we're kind of stuck. And Jeralyn is probably the only one who can convince them to sign off. She used a lot of her influence getting them to OK the hospitalization last fall. I've talked to a lot of people about Robin and she seems like a kid in danger of falling through the cracks through no fault of her own. Tough circumstances."

"Maybe so, but other people see her as having some kind of special arrangement and they don't like it," Patrazzo added.

"I get that, Pat, but a girl like Robin *deserves* some special arrangements. I had one of the Kessler High counselors come down and talk to her, but she's really slow to open up and trust anyone. I'd like to find a teacher she connects with. An *advocate*. I'm just not sure who."

"Maybe there's a kid who could help," Watters wondered. "Does she have any friends? You started that Pinicon Pal thing for the new kids. Maybe she could use some kind of peer helper."

"I probably haven't done a very good job communicating what is going on with her to faculty. I'll try to do that this afternoon and ask if anyone thinks they can connect with her or knows of a student who might. Thanks for the reminder and the conversation, guys. This is one of those things you don't look up in a book."

LET'S FORM A COMMITTEE

Joe had mixed emotions about the conference principals meetings. On one hand, he knew they were valuable learning and networking opportunities. He always brought back a new idea, contact, or resource after attending. Plus, listening to his colleagues vent and share stories reminded him that the grass is not always greener on another principal's side of the fence.

Valuable though they were, he often had trouble making the meetings. They were typically held at 10 a.m. in a district about forty minutes away. That meant that Joe would get the day started, have a few things pop up, and often miss his departure time. A second problem was that, as he and the other principals liked to lament, they often spent the entire meeting checking their phones and solving problems on the drive home.

To address this, Joe had suggested making it a 7:30 a.m. breakfast meeting. That, he said, would keep early morning events from getting in the way of attendance since the principals would be on their way before anyone arrived at school. There was interest in his idea, though Joe sensed some were reluctant to act on a rookie's suggestion.

Discussing the racial tension and the Pinicon-Piedmont game and Joe's earlier conversation with Piedmont High School Principal Fred Pruitt was on the January agenda, and Joe made sure to arrive early. When it was his turn to speak, he could tell that most of the other principals were familiar with what had happened at the game. Some agreed that the conference needed to address fan behavior and, more specifically, fans with painted faces. Others agreed with Pruitt—that there was no major problem, other than perhaps some overly sensitive Pinicon players, parents, and principal.

One from the latter group had reviewed the sportsmanship ratings of schools in the league, along with the aggregate ratings compared to other conferences in the state. One principal said he could identify with Joe's position, but also pointed out that Piedmont's overall sportsmanship ratings had been higher than both Pinicon and Kessler the previous year. He then suggested that, given this fact, maybe the problem was more with the Kessler-turned-Pinicon kids than with Piedmont or other schools.

Joe was livid but disguised his frustration. He thanked the group for the data and discussion. "The averages are fine, but there's a major difference," he noted. "The figures are from *last year*. Pinicon didn't have any minority students to speak of. So in a very real sense, that was then and this is now."

"Well, Joe, the numbers show what happened was an isolated incident. No need to make a big deal out of it. I say we watch things closely, see what happens, and deal with it if needed," said LeRoy Moore from Greenville High. Fred Pruitt nodded in agreement.

"The numbers do show a positive picture, LeRoy. So do *averages* about school shootings, but don't we all review them every time there's an *isolated incident* on the news?" Joe asked.

"Now we're talking apples and oranges," said Blake Howard from South Valley High.

Pete Hooper from Eagle Center High disagreed. "We've gotta be in this together, Blake. If one school has this issue at a league game, we've all got to address it together. That's why we're in a *conference*."

This prompted more discussion on both sides. Joe pressed his case further. "I'm willing to bet if this involved kids who had been around a long time, it would seem different. Is there some particular length of time kids have to be in a school before they're full members? I'm not aware of a *waiting period* before our values and bylaws are supposed to kick in. Let's not make *my new kids* the problem. They didn't do anything wrong. They just showed up to play. I've yet to have anyone tell me what they did wrong, unless maybe it's raising an issue no one wants to talk about."

The group talked in circles for a few more minutes. When one principal said he was frustrated at spending so much time on the topic when the league's overall sportsmanship ratings were high, several agreed and said they should move on to more pressing and academic issues. Joe countered and said how proud he was of the sportsmanship shown by the Pinicon players who let Tommy Bauer score in the closing seconds of the Pinicon-Sherwood game.

"I'm not calling *that* an isolated incident. I'm holding it up as an example of what's right with our activities programs. But we don't seem willing to look at *other evidence*, the rest of the story. It's like we're so high on the good averages that we're sticking our head in the sand on stuff that's not so pretty. I'm not gonna ignore it."

As soon as the words were out of his mouth, he wondered if he had come across too strong. But he felt good. The buckeye in his pocket reminded him of the way Professor Summers and Elton Rash, his colorful grandfather, approached things—assertive and direct. There were certainly times when he was just that. But his attempts at directness had sometimes come across as combative or overly aggressive, such as his tense exchanges with Patrazzo and Petersen in the fall semester.

In the end, the conference principals voted to "form a committee of ADs to monitor sportsmanship closely" for the rest of the year and give a report to the principals in May.

Claire called on Joe's way back to Pinicon. "How'd it go?"

"Not sure I accomplished anything. They're basically doing nothing. Not sure if they don't want to listen to a rookie or if they just don't get it. I hate to think some are a little prejudiced, but who knows. It was kind of like Congress. They passed the buck and formed a committee of ADs to study sportsmanship."

Hearing those words, Joe was reminded of another of Professor Summers's quips. *A committee is often a dark alley where we send good ideas to be ambushed and killed.* He hoped that was not the case. Just then, his phone rang again, this time with an unfamiliar number coming across the screen. It was Judy Christensen, the principal at Fox Valley High School.

"Joe, I just want to tell you I thought you did a great job today. I know the group didn't seem real receptive, but sometimes the old boys club needs a little shaking up. Leave it to a woman and a rookie to understand that! I didn't say a lot today and I pick my times pretty carefully in those meetings, but you have more support than you know. Just stick with it."

Joe thanked her for the affirmation. Unlike many times when he was on the phone solving problems that had come up while he was away, he and Judy talked about the challenges and opportunities of the principalship. Talking to a new ally principal felt good.

"Issues like the one you raised this morning are so frustrating," she said. "But the beauty of the job is that we have the opportunity to raise them and address them, sometimes for the first time. I love being able to do that. And you seem pretty good at it, for a rookie," she teased.

QUESTIONS

1. What practical ideas do you have for how principals can protect personal and family time?
2. Should Heidi Morris attend the Empowering Educators Conference as a new substitute teacher?
3. React to Joe's desire to change his approach with Richards.
4. Evaluate Joe's handling of the scene in Petersen's PE class.
5. Should Joe respond to concerns about special treatment for Robin Stiles?
6. Principals seeking support from each other is essential, both personally and professionally. Evaluate Joe's approach at the principals' meeting.

Chapter Two

Late January

Reaching Out

WORTH A TRY

Joe was relieved that Mace Stallworth had not caused any more disruptions since attacking Henry Miller in October. Still, he always seemed to be on edge. After Joe had suspended Mace from the bus indefinitely, special education teacher Carole Martinson warned Joe that he couldn't keep Mace off the bus forever. Joe transported Mace himself for the initial period of Mace's in-school suspension before Gregg Altman unexpectedly offered a solution.

"I know this has been a pain. Since I go right by his trailer park on the way to early morning driver's ed, why don't we put a school bus sign on the back of the car and I'll bring him?" he asked. "He could probably use someone dragging him out of bed anyway." Though Mace's attendance wasn't great and Mace and his mother sometimes failed to answer when Altman banged on the door, he was usually successful at rousting Mace out and getting him to school.

The arrangement made sense, and Altman had good relationships with most kids. At the very least, it was a consistent way for Mace to get to school. At the very best, Altman might be able to build some kind of rapport with Mace and prevent him from boiling over.

In the meantime, Joe had spent a fair amount of time looking through Mace's file from Kessler. His Individualized Education Plan showed only academic goals. His grades at Kessler had been decent. Attendance and outbursts of violence seemed to be the biggest issues. Martinson told Joe that she had few problems with Mace in her classroom but worried that Mace and other teachers got on "like oil and water."

Joe had tried to maintain regular contact with Mace's mother, Lorna, though his calls often went unanswered. He had tried a couple of times to catch her by stopping by her trailer on his way home from meetings at Kessler. Sometimes, she answered the door. At others, he was sure she was home but wouldn't answer. On a cold gray afternoon after a technology meeting at Kessler, Joe caught Lorna at home, apparently sober and in a good mood.

"Mrs. Martinson and I have looked at Mace's IEP quite a bit and talked with his teachers and the bus driver. I think it would be good to get together and talk about how we can help him."

"If you bring the papers out I'll sign them," she said. "That's what we done last year."

"There's always paperwork, but the most important thing is for us to *talk about* what's going on. When Mace is at school and under control, he does OK. It's attendance and going off that's the problem. We need to get our heads around that and see what *Mace* thinks."

"I always said the boy ain't dumb. He's just crazy, like his dad. I'll come and talk about him, but I need a way to get there and back," she said.

"That's usually not something we can do, but if you'll promise to come, we'll figure out a way to get you there. And we're gonna have Mace at the meeting, too. This is his deal, not just a bunch of us sitting around talking about him."

"Well, I hope he don't go crazy in the meeting, but I'll keep my thumb on him."

'Cause that works so well, Joe said to himself, glancing at the holes Mace had punched in the trailer wall. He thanked her and promised to be in touch soon about the meeting. He wondered if Mace's IEP had really been handled by someone just getting Lorna's signature on a stack of documents in the past.

ROLE REVERSAL

Joe had promised students and staff that he would go through a student's day before the year was through. He had promoted it when speaking to civic clubs, included it in his blog and column in *The Pinicon Herald*, and even suggested that parents and community members consider shadowing a student, though some members of the leadership team said many teachers were lukewarm on the idea.

"I get that," Joe said. "But the fact is, it's their school too, not just ours. The *invitation* is more important than whether anyone actually takes us up on it."

Jeralyn, who was finally back to work following her surgery, had joined Carrie in teasing that Joe was on the verge of turning Pinicon into a reality TV show with things like his student-shadowing idea. Through all the questions and teasing, Joe insisted it was a good idea. Jeralyn urged him to limit eligibility to students with a 3.0 grade point average. Joe disagreed and ultimately sided with the leadership team, which felt that if Joe wanted a truly authentic experience, he should put no restrictions on eligibility.

Joe hyped the drawing during his lunches with students, in the daily announcements, and at every other opportunity. He and the leadership team shared a laugh when Rhonda Prior said, "You're assuming that the kids might think it's *cool* to have the principal shadowing them. And that might be far from the truth!"

Joe asked Becky Marks, the charismatic student council president, to draw the name in his office on a Friday afternoon. Teachers Martha Mills and Gregg Altman made the drawing available for viewing via the network in classrooms. Becky pulled Kendrick Wallace's name and invited him to the office to pick up his $50 gift card to King's Clothing in Pinicon. Joe welcomed Kendrick to the office and reminded him that the purpose of the exercise was for him to experience a student's day at school.

For Kendrick Wallace, the day began early. The junior member of the band and football team was the oldest son of an energetic single mom, Deb, who opened the Quik Mart Convenience Store every morning at 5:30 a.m. This meant Kendrick was responsible for getting his middle and elementary school siblings ready for school. Joe was surprised and delighted when Kendrick's mom called to suggest he start his day at their house when Kendrick started getting the kids ready. Joe wondered if he was in for more than he bargained for when Kendrick said Joe should met him in the weight room at 5:15 *and then* head home to get the kids ready for school.

Joe asked Carrie and Jeralyn if it seemed a little weird for him to be going to the house while Kendrick got his siblings ready for school.

"Maybe, but you put it out there and the family seems like they're all over it," Jeralyn said.

On shadow day, Joe met Kendrick at 5:15 in the weight room and headed home with him at 6:30 to get his siblings ready. By 7:30, Kendrick had made their lunches and gotten them to school. Joe followed him through a full day of classes, concluding with band ensemble practice after school followed by a couple hours of unloading a truck and stocking some shelves at the Quik Mart. Joe loved the experience and the insight it gave him into everything from the way teachers engage students, to how busy students' lives are, not to mention how tired he was at the end of the day.

Several teachers presented unexpectedly engaging lessons. He found himself captivated by Helen McCallister's reading of a section of *A Farewell to Arms,* thoroughly lost in Rhonda Prior's Algebra II class, and wondering if he might have become interested in architecture had he been able to take something like Frank Young's Computer-Aided Design when he was in high school. Larry Den Herder's petri dishes teeming with nasty things swabbed from surfaces around school made him more of a germophobe than he already was.

He was also surprised by how quickly he morphed into the student's role. Many seemed to forget the principal was sitting next to Kendrick's desk. Other aspects of the day surprised him, like how he wasn't yet hungry for lunch at 11:10 a.m. and how he had almost no time to go to the bathroom. He intentionally took the wrong book to Joyce Barry's class, knowing that she refused to let students leave if they were missing something and assigned a zero for class participation. She seemed uncomfortable telling Joe he would receive no participation points for the day and that he couldn't leave to get the right book.

"But he hasn't even had a *chance* to participate yet," Kendrick and other students protested.

Perhaps that would open a door of discussion. All of this would be great material for his blog, the next faculty meeting, and his own reflection.

EMPOWERED

By all accounts, the Empowering Educators Conference had been a smashing success. The teams from Kessler and Pinicon returned to school energized and armed with practical suggestions for sharing what they had learned. This was music to Joe's ears, along with the fact that the conference keynote focused on the importance of a unified vision, which was consistent with his emphasis on defining the Pinicon Way. He remembered attending conferences and returning with the same energy, only to find that the good ideas started to fade as soon as he got back into the school routine. He was determined to help the team maintain the momentum.

The teachers who had attended the Empowering Educators Conference seemed convinced that they had a way to do that. Within a week of returning, they began sharing short tidbits of ideas for increasing student engagement and streamlining curriculum through sending e-mails, writing short notes on neon green paper in mailboxes, posting several times a week on TeachShare, and launching a YouTube channel aimed at Pinicon staff. They each offered informal early morning and after school overviews of things they had learned. Rhonda Prior joked that the team was "carpet bombing" the Pinicon staff with ideas.

Joe was energized to hear the team strategize about how they might "target" specific people on the Pinicon staff to join them in exploring some interdisciplinary teaching that would cross traditional course or department boundaries. Their idea was to settle on one or two areas and then work through potential cross-curricular connections. Joe had hoped that sending newcomer Heidi Morris to the conference wouldn't be viewed negatively by the teachers. It appeared as though she was fully immersed in the plans.

Watters asked Joe if he thought it was too soon to launch the effort. Joe said he liked the idea of starting new initiatives like this with a coalition of the willing. "I don't want to overload you or the rest of the staff, but if you wait too long, the momentum might be lost. I think you're going at it about right. And don't be shy about what you need from me in terms of support."

Joe was thrilled that the team asked him to sit in on their planning sessions, where he tried to simply watch and listen, though it was hard not to jump in and share his own ideas. Hard as it was to hang back, he told himself and the team that it was important that anything that came from their attendance at the conference be "teacher driven."

He thought this might be his best work in instructional leadership and he wasn't even doing it *directly*. It reminded him of Kristi saying instructional leadership takes many forms. "I'm trying to offer support and let things take shape," he told Zylstra. "Allowing us flexibility, getting these folks to the conference, and hiring Heidi Morris are game changers. It's amazing to see what we can do with some resources, and I want to thank you for that."

"What you're really talking about is leading by creating the right conditions," Zylstra said. "And this is probably ahead of schedule. I know Kessler High is having some similar conversations, but things are moving more slowly there. That might be because they have so many other initiatives going. The superintendent probably needs to scale a few back," she laughed. "Like Michael Fullan says, we can only handle a couple at a time."

"It's been a long time since teachers here had professional opportunities like this," Joe said. "I hope all this can become the new normal and the way we do things here. The Pinicon Way. *That* would be cool."

"It's great that the teachers asked you to sit in on their planning sessions. That shows that some trust is growing. And don't be too shy about sharing your ideas. If they didn't want them, they wouldn't have asked you to sit in," Zylstra suggested. "Protect that time and be sure you get there."

MARRIAGE COUNSELING

Joe was struggling to keep his eyes open wading through the new state manual on tracking annual yearly progress for required state tests when Carrie peeked her head in. "Diane Watters is here. Do you have a few minutes?"

"Sure," said Joe, happy for any sort of reprieve from the testing manual. He had met Mark Watters's wife in the fall and chatted with her at ballgames.

He welcomed her into his office and offered her a seat at the round table. "Thanks," she said. "Do you mind if I close the door?"

Diane began by saying how much Mark had enjoyed the Empowering Educators Conference. "For the last several years, a lot of teachers have felt like they were going it alone. He really appreciates the focus on teaching you've brought." Joe said he was glad to hear that and added that Mark was a key part of the leadership of the building.

Diane seemed not to be listening. She straightened her shoulders in the chair and lifted her chin. "Joe, I came to tell you something that you need to know. I hate to do it, but not saying anything will only lead to bigger problems, and I have no choice."

Joe's mind was suddenly racing, small talk pleasantries having evaporated. "OK," he said cautiously.

"I'm not sure how much you know about Heidi Morris," she began. "I know she's a good teacher, energetic and everything, but there are some other things you need to know."

Joe could feel his brow furrow, trying to anticipate where Diane was headed.

"I'll get right to it. She's got an eye for some of the male teachers here. Have you seen the way she flaunts herself?"

Joe said that he hadn't.

"So it will probably be news to you that when she, Mark, and Gregg Altman were driving to the airport for the conference she was breast pumping," Diane said, hands and voice now shaking. "And if she was doing that on the way, who knows what else happened at the conference in Orlando!"

Joe was off-balance. "By breast pumping, you mean . . ."

"She's nursing her baby, so I guess a few miles down the road she started pumping. What kind of woman does that? Why can't she do it at home? Or at the airport? She clearly planned it so she could unbutton her blouse with two men in the front seat. If she's starved for attention because her husband is always gone and she's in that big house alone, that's her business. But don't go sleazing around other people's husbands! Why didn't she ride with the other women? How convenient . . . no peeking, guys, while I unbutton my blouse! I'm telling you, she's a predator!"

"I can see that you're upset," Joe said, sliding the Kleenex box toward her. "How did this come up?"

"She posted on Facebook that she was going to the conference and needed to pump or she was gonna explode. A friend of a friend showed me. It's bad enough that she flaunts herself, but she has to brag about it on Facebook too?" Diane questioned why a substitute would even be sent to the conference and wondered how and why Heidi wound up in the car with her husband and Altman instead of riding with Carole Martinson and Allison Jesup.

She looked directly at Joe and said in a soft voice, "Mark and I have our issues, like every couple, but I'm going to protect my marriage. I'm going to make sure she understands that and stays the hell away from my husband."

Joe asked if Mark knew she was coming to talk to him. Diane said he did not. "Diane, thank you for letting me know. I'm sure it is awkward and uncomfortable. I have to talk with Heidi and Mark. I know of no issues or problems. That doesn't mean there aren't any. *I'll* talk with Heidi. I don't want you talking to her. Will you agree to that?"

After a long pause, Diane said she would. After an uncomfortable silence and several shallow breaths, she stood, extended her hand, and thanked Joe for seeing her. She left quickly and without responding to Carrie's goodbye.

Exhaling, Joe leaned back in his chair. *It's so true*, he thought to himself, *that you can't make this stuff up*. He dialed Zylstra's mobile number, hoping to catch her between meetings. No luck. Next, he began dialing Professor Summers before remembering that he and his wife were spending a few weeks in Costa Rica. Adhering to his rule that the less he interacted with Mitchell, the better, he sent Cal Murphy a text asking him to call when he had a chance. He thought about asking McHale for advice, but thought better of it, as his wife and Diane were members of the same church choir and good friends.

He began working on a handout for the school board, outlining the results of the Empowering Educators Conference, when Carrie reminded him that he was supposed to be in McCallister's Great Books class for the first meeting of the students and community members who were reading *The Things They Carried*. He shook his head at how he could so look forward to time in classrooms and nearly miss it because of other things. It was a good thing Carrie watched his schedule so closely.

STUCK IN THE MIDDLE

The time in McCallister's class passed quickly. McCallister chatted with students and parents, many of whom didn't strike Joe as avid readers. He realized how much he enjoyed the role of student and completely forgot about the shocking visit from Diane Watters.

He had read the first few pages of the assigned book before falling asleep a few nights before. That reminded him of how Professor Summers advised principals to always be reading a good novel. "Even if you only have ten minutes a day, it's ten minutes of escape and your mind is going to need that." He hoped being involved would provide such an escape and a chance to engage with students and the community at the same time.

After thanking the parents, grandparents, and community members who would also be reading the book, he headed back to his office. He decided to ask Sutt and Kristi how to proceed with Diane Watters's complaint. Sutt answered, but Joe got no response from Kristi. "You got five minutes?"

"Sure, cowboy. Is this a nice surprise or a crisis line call?"

"I'll let you decide."

Sutt couldn't keep from laughing. "I'm sorry, man, but that's funny. I have no idea what to tell you. *Zero*. I'm glad it's not me, because I'd have to hand the whole thing off to somebody else."

"Yeah, well *I* don't have anybody to hand it to." Joe admired Sutt's often-lighthearted approach to things. It wasn't that he didn't care or was unprofessional, but he seemed less vulnerable to the emotional stress of the job. Professor Summers had said that today's *crisis* is often a *funny story* five years later and that leaders had to be empathetic but not too emotionally tied to daily crises. The situation with Diane Watters might seem funny at some point in the future, but it didn't feel so to Joe at the moment.

"I guess you bring them in separately and ask if the story is accurate. If it is, tell her how stupid and unprofessional it was. Does she think she's one of the guys or something? Is she a flirt like the guy's wife says?" Sutt asked.

"She seems really comfortable with everyone and I don't think she flirts, but it still seems weird. But Claire nursed our kids, and I know how tough that is. There were times when she was miserable."

"So talk to them, document it, and tell them to make sure it doesn't impact their jobs. And watch what she puts on Facebook." Kristi said. "The whole Facebook post was really dumb."

"Remember how Summers said nothing good ever happens in the bleachers?" Joe asked. "I'm ready to say that nothing good ever happens on Facebook."

Sutt snickered. "So you don't want Pinicon teachers using a Facebook page for classes? I'm sorry, dude. I'm picturing you talking to the guy's wife, who is coming uncorked."

"I know. I wasn't ready for that one. I feel like I'm being pulled into the middle of something I want nothing to do with, but have no choice," Joe said.

Sutt changed the subject and shared a situation his principal, Rudy Carlson, asked him to handle. "If it makes you feel any better, I just got back from meeting the manager of a McDonald's. We've got a bus driver who demands free food when he stops his activity bus. Been doing it all over this part of the state for sports trips, field trips, choir, you name it. All the fast food places hate him 'cause he orders eight or ten bucks worth of stuff and then says it is free because he's the driver. Gets all pissed off if they want him to pay. Several managers called our transportation guy, who did nothing. Then it got to the super and to Rudy. No idea why Rudy made me handle it. Anyway, he would only stop the bus where he could get free food. The cholesterol smorgasbord is over, though. We just fired him."

"Sutt, I've gotta go. My superintendent's on the phone and she's about to hear the breast-pumping story. I'll see what she wants me to do. I wish Kristi had answered. Anyway, let's talk soon."

Zylstra asked if there were any performance problems with either Watters or Morris. "None. Heidi Morris is brand new and just the sub, but she and Mark Watters are two of our best, which is why I sent them to the conference in the first place."

"OK. Actually, I don't think it's that big of a deal. You can go to the mall today and see a woman nursing a baby. Some people are too uptight, but I won't get into all that." Zylstra suggested bringing Watters and Morris in and letting each know that Mark's wife had come in upset and to make sure that none of this impacted their teaching. "You should also tell Morris that posting it on Facebook is a really bad idea. And of course, document, document, document."

Joe thanked her for calling him back and hung up. Then he realized that he was twenty minutes late for a scheduled observation in Stu Petersen's PE class.

A MENTOR'S GUIDANCE

McHale's advice for how to approach Heidi Morris and Mark Watters was the same as Zylstra's, which was reassuring. Joe also wanted ideas on teachers getting engaged in examining students' test scores without having them feel that merely improving scores was Joe's end goal. McHale had previously said that he doubted whether Pinicon Secondary teachers had done much in this area. "We do it all the time in elementary in our grade-level teams, but I know it's a harder sell in middle and high school," McHale said, encouraging Joe to also consult with Murphy at Kessler High.

"My first thought is to find out how familiar your teachers are with what's even on the tests. I doubt they know much about them. With all the local, state, and national curriculum stuff that's flying around, you've got a multi-year project on your hands. My only caution would be making sure you're not overloading them. Moving forward with stuff from the Empowering Educators Conference is gonna be a lot of work and I know you're also working on the Pinicon Way thing. Don't give them too much at once," McHale advised.

"That's hard, especially when I keep finding things that haven't been done but are really important. At times, I have a hard time prioritizing," he confided.

"Maybe you can do some of the testing stuff with a subcommittee or department that wants to focus on their subject. That might plant the seed and get the others thinking about their own areas. Maybe it involves everyone next year," McHale speculated.

Joe said he would pursue the subcommittee or department idea before raising his third question. "I've been reading this blog about how legislators don't know much about schools but are the ones passing all the laws and basically acting like they do."

"Yep. Everyone's an expert because they went to school. The politicians' party headquarters give them a list of things to talk about and vote for," McHale said. "But, I hate to be so cynical."

"You're right, though. Anyway, the author says we should invite legislators to come to school whenever we have the chance. I've had a couple of calls from state reps about the Pinicon-Kessler sharing arrangement and we just had the teachers come back from the conference. What would you think about giving our reps an invitation to spend a day in each of our schools? The blog author calls it *Making Them Say No*, as in challenging them to actually show up or say they won't or can't."

McHale liked the idea. "Call Cal Murphy at Kessler. I'll bet he'd love it too."

Joe took McHale's advice and dialed Murphy. While his to-do list was packed, he also knew that ideas like this often fell out of mind if not acted upon at the right time.

"Joe, I got your text earlier, but I've been in a special ed staffing all morning. Sorry," Murphy said. Joe had forgotten that he had also wanted to get Murphy's take on the breast-pumping situation. After conceding that he hadn't heard of anything like it before, he offered essentially the same advice as Zylstra and McHale.

Murphy was intrigued by Joe's idea of inviting area legislators to Pinicon and Kessler to experience a day at school and learn more about the sharing arrangement. "Honestly, that's not something I've done a very good job of, so I'm glad you brought it up. I think we should give it a shot. Maybe we could pick a day when teachers are doing some good professional learning so they could see what that's about. And we could show how TeachShare works, too."

"Yeah. A normal day and some professional learning would be perfect," Joe said.

"Assuming there is such a thing as a *normal day*," Murphy quipped.

"You got me there. Maybe we could do it on one of those constituent days when they are supposed to be back home talking to people. I'd like to invite them to take the state tests while they're here, but that might be going a little too far."

"I love it. I remember a press conference where a reporter asked a governor a question from the sophomore test and he tanked it. That's bad PR, but what a conversation starter if legislators would actually do it," Murphy said.

"Absolutely. And throw in some board members, business owners, police chiefs, farmers, stay-at-home moms," Joe laughed. "I'm about half serious. Maybe we should push that."

AN AWKWARD PLACE

"This is really awkward," Joe told Heidi Morris, explaining that Diane Watters had been to see him. "Were you breast pumping on the way to the airport for the Empowering Educators Conference?"

Heidi's eyes widened. "Well, yeah. Rhonda called and said the roads were getting bad and we should leave right away. I was scrambling to get ready and didn't have time at home. I don't know how much you know about breast-feeding, but..."

"I know it's not easy. Claire nursed our kids," Joe said, remembering bad weather on the day the two groups headed to the airport.

"I would have done it at home, but we left early and there wasn't time. I was in the back and had a blanket. Joe, I hope you don't think I'm inappropriate or something. I was riding with those guys so we could talk about our TeachShare stuff. And believe me, feeling like a human milk wagon is not a lot of fun. And Diane coming in here like I'm after her husband... it's about to push me over the edge," she said, tears welling in her eyes.

"OK, this is a bad situation," Joe said, sliding the same Kleenex box he had offered to Diane Watters across the table. "We have to keep this from impacting your job, Mark's job. Diane might have been upset regardless, but saying something on Facebook was a really bad idea."

"I post stuff about the baby all the time. In fact, I'm in a couple breast-feeding support groups on Facebook. It helps a lot. This sounds terrible, but I think Mark's wife has her own issues."

"I don't know anything about that, but I want you to think carefully about what you post and potential ramifications. It's different for us as teachers."

An hour later, Joe stopped by Watters's classroom. Joe admired Watters's creativity as a teacher and propensity to ask questions. He felt they had a good relationship, but Joe felt awkward wading into the conversation.

Joe slid into a student desk in Watters's classroom after pulling the door shut. "Mark, I need to ask you about the trip to the Empowering Educators conference," Joe said.

"Yeah. Well worth the time and money, as I told you. Best thing I've ever been to."

"Specifically, the trip to the airport."

Mark looked perplexed. "Snowy. Great conversation on the way down, except for some white knuckle driving with the ice," he said, nodding.

Joe asked if Morris had been breast pumping in the car. Watters's shoulders sunk and he let out a sigh. "That? Yeah, she was. Said she didn't have time before and was dying since we left early. Am I sensing an ugly Pinicon rumor?"

"Diane came to see me and was pretty upset. She felt like it was inappropriate and that maybe Heidi was . . . I don't know . . . flirting with you and Gregg. That it was intentional."

Watters sighed. "Jesus, Joe. Altman's the *single* one. I haven't thought once about it since that day! My eyes were on the road, for God's sake! Diane and I haven't even *talked* about it. Am I in some kind of trouble?"

"You're not in trouble, Mark. I'm just following up. One never knows what's going to come through the door. The most important thing is that you and Heidi—*everyone*—keeps doing a great job in class and that nothing distracts from that. It's no good for anyone if there is the perception of something else going on."

Watters cocked his head slightly. "Are you saying you think there's something going on between me and Heidi?"

"No. I'm saying perceptions and rumors are tough in schools. *Any* school. Your wife is obviously upset and that's between the two of you. My interest is to be sure that none of this impacts your teaching. Or Heidi's. That's it."

Joe tried to lighten the mood with some small talk about other things and class projects, but it was clear that Watters's mind was elsewhere, so Joe cut it short. "Let me know if you need anything or if we need to talk about this some more," Joe offered.

RISING TEMPS

Each week, Joe blocked an uninterrupted hour with Jeralyn on his calendar. Their private chats were open to any topic either wanted to raise. He liked to tease her that she was a good source for what was being said in the teacher's lounge. The worn sofa in her office creaked as Joe dropped onto it, perhaps a little too hard.

"I'm worried about our climate, Joe," Jeralyn said.

"When you were in the hospital, I told you to double your meds and get back here quickly. Look what happened. It took longer than you thought and our climate fell apart," he joked.

"I'm serious. People are on edge. I feel like we're getting to an us-versus-them environment, mostly with the Kessler transfers. God knows it could be hard to be new and different here. I worry about the minority kids, the special ed kids. And there's this special treatment nonsense. Somehow people got all caught up in Javaris Hayes being a homecoming candidate, Robin Stiles's escorts and spot in the office, the free physicals, the Confederate flags, the article in the paper. I haven't felt this before."

"That special treatment thing is a joke," Joe snapped. "If anyone is getting special treatment, it's *Pinicon* people who've been here a long time! How would they like to try . . ."

Jeralyn cut him off. "Perception, Joe. We're talking about how things are *seen and interpreted*. It doesn't seem like anything to us because we're knee-deep in it."

"Knee-deep? Try neck-deep! I don't get what the hell . . ." Joe said, shaking his head.

"Just listen, Joe. Take a breath. Your honeymoon as principal is over. We're coming into February, which is a tough time of year. There's goofy stuff out there."

He was aware of the special treatment perception, but hadn't shared Jeralyn's level of concern. But he was no longer communicating with the Pinicon Pals regularly, and his interaction with most of the Kessler transfer students was irregular at best.

"I know checking in with the new kids was intended to help and it probably did. But others see it as special treatment and favoritism. And when you *stopped*, I think some of the new kids felt like they lost that person who was really looking out for them," Jeralyn said.

"So my attention to certain kids who need support looks like special treatment and backing off makes them feel like I've abandoned them," Joe summarized, shrugging his shoulders. "I'm damned either way. So what do we do?"

"Let me send a few kids to you. You're approachable. Get them talking. Tell them you want to catch up and see how things are going. They'll tell you. And we'll go from there. Make sense?"

WHERE DO I SIGN?

On the heels of Jeralyn pointing out the special treatment perception, Joe regretted the timing of his promise to provide Lorna Stallworth with transportation to Mace's IEP meeting. At the same time, he was committed to following through on the promise and getting her to the meeting, especially since she had simply signed whatever papers were brought to her when Mace was enrolled at Kessler. "Giving her a ride is a little above and beyond what a lot of schools would do, but we're not other schools. And without getting together, there's no chance of making any progress," Joe said. "So I'll get her here, *this* time."

Joe told Martinson that she should lead the meeting. "You're the special ed expert and you know Mace best. I also get the sense that Lorna will respond better to a woman. I'll jump in whenever I need to," Joe said.

Martinson did a masterful job of reviewing Mace's situation. Without directly saying Kessler had mishandled his IEP, she made it clear that the team didn't think it reflected Mace's needs. Her explanation was in plain English and informal, but Joe still worried that Mace and Lorna's attention was drifting. *They've probably been through this a thousand times,* Joe thought, *and nothing ever changes.*

Martinson and the teachers reviewed Mace's work in their classes, which all pointed to attendance and anger issues being a larger problem than his cognitive ability. After each teacher had spoken, Martinson said, "I think we should ask Mace what he thinks of all this."

"Oh, you don't wanna go there," Lorna rasped. "We might see that anger y'all been talking about."

"Actually, Lorna, we do wanna hear from Mace. He's the reason we're here, and we need to know where he's at with all this," Joe said.

"Well, y'all asked for it." She looked at Mace. "You gonna say something or just sit there?"

Mace fidgeted in his chair, and Joe wondered if he was about to explode. If he did, the hope of coming out of the meeting with a positive feeling about a new IEP focused on behavioral and attendance goals, rather than the ill-conceived academic goals from Kessler, would evaporate. Joe worried the team might conclude that, even though the October bus incident had been Mace's only real blowup, Pinicon couldn't meet his needs. It might be that the at-risk/alternative program at Kessler was a better match, but it was full and Joe wanted to try things at Pinicon first.

Over the next several minutes, Martinson and Kramer put on a clinic for getting a student to open up. Without pushing too hard, they posed gentle questions that got Mace talking. His answers aligned with what the team had concluded coming into the meeting—that Mace was struggling with impulse and anger control that often caused him to skip school.

Over the next forty minutes, the team put together a plan that included some testing by the regional school psychologist and new IEP goals aimed specifically at Mace's attendance and anger control. It allowed for Mace to have some "cooldown" space if he felt himself getting agitated. Lorna seemed fascinated by the team's discussion.

"I've spoken to Ernie Johansen, the bus driver. He knows we're meeting today and he said that he's fine with Mace returning to the bus on a trial basis," Joe said.

This time Mace spoke up quickly and without hesitation. "Can I just keep riding with Mr. Altman? He's cool and I like him."

"I have no problem with that," Joe said. *That Altman is a kid magnet,* Joe thought to himself. *I wonder if we could ever find the money to hire him as an at-risk coordinator.*

The meeting ended with the standard documents being signed. Lorna Stallworth seemed unusually upbeat and chatty, especially with Martinson. "Are you any relation to the Martinsons over in Cosgrove?"

That has to be the first small talk Lorna Stallworth has had with a teacher in a long time, Joe thought. *She's had a lot of teachers talk at her, but not many talk with her.* Martinson and Jeralyn were waiting in his office when he got back from running Lorna and Mace home.

"Ladies, *that* was awfully good. Thank you. You were *masterful*," he said.

"It was kind of amazing," Martinson agreed. "I'm not sure they've ever been in a meeting where there was actual discussion *about Mace*."

Joe and Jeralyn agreed. "He still might punch Gregg Altman in the mouth on their way to school tomorrow. But this was progress and we have a chance with him. Good job, folks," Jeralyn said.

SKYPE CONFERENCE

Joe was anxious to share the seemingly positive outcome of Mace's IEP meeting.

"You're doing a good job, Joe. Sounds like the system has failed that family for a while. It's a good example of how the process has to be about the kiddo and not the paperwork. The past is the best predictor of future behavior, so he may be coming around if he's only had the one blowup last fall," Kristi said.

Kristi's positive feedback made Joe feel good because of the respect he had for her. "We'll see, Kristi, but I appreciate that, coming from you."

"Well, OHS is in an uproar since we talked last," Sutt announced. "We just fired a guy who's taught here for twelve years. Remember the sub who was blogging about all the bad stuff she sees in schools? She was subbing for us and found a notebook with a steamy story about a teacher/student relationship. She brought it straight to me; I took it to Rudy and he went straight to HR."

Joe's and Kristi's eyes widened.

"Rudy and HR determined he was lying. The girl, *a freshman*, said not everything in the story is true, but that they were in a relationship. She had all kinds of creepy text messages from the dude. Really weird."

Kristi wondered if it was true that inappropriate teacher/student relationships are far more common than most people realize. Joe suspected they are, citing a couple high-profile cases in the news.

"But it gets worse," Sutt said. "When we brought the girl's parents in to tell them, they said they thought that scumbag and their daughter would be *real good together* and they had been hoping things would work out. This is their fifteen-year-old daughter! How's that for a ticket on the crazy train?"

"I've got a couple passengers for you," Kristi said. "We do a trivia-night fundraiser with parents, like a game show. Long story short, I had to step between two dads who were ready to fight because one accused the other of cheating. Said he was looking up answers on his phone."

"He's competitive and resourceful! Big deal! Were they really gonna go?" Sutt asked.

"I think so. I stepped between them and was looking at their sternums when I kicked them both out. An off-duty sheriff's deputy followed me out to make sure everything was OK. She was watching from a distance and decided one of the dads was drunk. She called it in and he ended up getting busted right in the parking lot. Worst part was that his son was one of the student workers and saw the whole thing. Poor kid."

"The stuff that goes on *amazes* me, and yet not much of it *surprises* me anymore, because I know just about anything's possible," Joe said.

"That's a good way to put it," Kristi said. "Making sure the crazy stuff doesn't knock us completely off balance like Summers always talked about is really the key," Kristi said.

"Amen, sister," Sutt scoffed.

QUESTIONS

1. Evaluate Joe's student shadow day. Is it a good use of his time? What, if anything, should come from it?
2. How should teachers be selected for attendance at professional conferences?
3. Diane Watters's visit placed Joe in an uncomfortable position. Evaluate his conversation with Heidi Morris and Mark Watters.
4. How should Joe respond to Jeralyn's concerns with the culture and climate at Pinicon?
5. Evaluate Mace Stallworth's IEP meeting. Has Joe overextended the school by providing transportation for Lorna and allowing Mace to continue to ride to school with Altman?

Chapter Three

Early February

Politics, Authenticity, and Support

IS IT WORTH IT?

"I need an update on TeachShare. It's an awful lot of money. Is it really worth it?" Mitchell asked over the phone. Joe wondered how Professor Summers or Elton Rash would respond, aware of the lucky buckeye in his pocket.

"Absolutely. Some are using it quite a bit. Others are slower, but that's to be expected."

"I'm just looking at budget. It's a helluva lot of money if only a few are using it. What's going on with Richards?"

"Richards is one of the main users. He's collaborating with a couple teachers in other states, working really hard. We meet several times a week. I also capped his enrollment, because that shop's awful small. He's got some tough kids but he's pretty good with them. They like him. We came down hard on a couple troublemakers and since then I'd say things are going pretty well."

"So what do you mean *meeting with him*?" Mitchell asked.

"We meet early in the morning, look at TeachShare, talk about curriculum, management, plans. Trying to build trust. I think I mishandled things for most of last semester. I'm trying to provide support, not just oversight and checking up all the time."

"You sure that's worth the time? You were going on about what a headache it was last fall. Teachers need to see you as the power figure. Authority."

Joe sighed. *How did a hacker like Don Mitchell rise to associate superintendent? What decade is he operating in?* "Actually, I think it's a perfect use of my time, and this kind of one-on-one work with teachers is the reason I got into this."

"So you have a different feeling from last fall? What happened to all your anger and concern? Are you going soft now?" Mitchell pressed.

A rush of anger-induced electricity shot through Joe's veins. "*Soft*? The issue isn't going soft. The issue is teachers *going it alone* for far too long. No shared leadership, not much attention to instruction from the principal. I'm trying to deliver on that, to offer support. I know management is important, but I'm hoping to get beyond that. I'm trying to lead, not run a police state. We're working hard down here, nobody more than Richards. We're moving forward."

"Fine, Joe, but let me remind you that you're young. Passionate. I like that. But you're not gonna save the world. We talked about management in your eval. You have to get that in order first. That's the priority. You can worry about leadership later."

"I'm glad you can feel some passion, Don," Joe said, taking his foot off the angry pedal. "I know I'm new and have a lot to learn. I'm trying to balance it, but do it my way. Thanks for the call," Joe said, desperately wanting to say more, but he didn't.

He hung up the phone frustrated and perplexed. He remembered talking about the adage of people rising in the organization to their own level of incompetence. It was hard to see how Mitchell held down the job as associate superintendent in a district like Kessler, let alone with a respected superintendent like Zylstra. But Mitchell was probably right about one thing. Joe needed to control what he could control. That didn't include Mitchell.

TRUTH TO POWER

Joe was surprised at how responsive the Kessler transfer students were to his questions about their comfort at Pinicon. Javaris Hayes said he didn't feel any overt hostility, but knew there were eyes upon him all the time. "Everybody thinks I came down here for sports. And so I kinda feel like the brown person jock. Like, some people wanna be seen with me 'cause I'm a novelty, but there's a barrier between us too. I'm never gonna get too close to them, but sports help."

Others described standoffish or cold treatment from many students and teachers. Like Javaris, few pointed to overt hostility. "It's more something you just feel, like stay in your place," said one freshman. "It's actually hard to explain to a white guy, and I don't mean that bad," she added quickly. Several mentioned how helpful their Pinicon Pal had been initially, but many said their Pals backed off after they learned their schedules and a few basics. "I think other people were mad at them if the Pals were *too nice* to us or something," one said. A couple related frustration at being addressed as a group. "Teachers will be like, 'Y'all better listen up and see how we do things here,' like we're from another country or something," said Richard Smith. Mace Stallworth said he was sure teachers thought he was responsible for everything that was missing, stolen, or damaged in the building. *Well, maybe you are*, Joe thought, before scolding himself.

When Joe asked why they hadn't formally communicated their concerns, most said they didn't want to add to the drama. Several said that they didn't feel entirely at home at Pinicon, yet it was better than being at Kessler or their former schools. "Better than Kessler is fine, but we want this to feel like home. Like you *belong*," Joe said.

A LITTLE TOO AUTHENTIC

Gregg Altman had done as much to apply and share what he had learned at the Empowering Educators Conference as anyone. He seemed to thrive on multitasking, four hours of sleep, and any extra duties that needed to be done, like getting Mace Stallworth to school. He connected well with a lot of students and his energy was infectious. Joe said this was a good thing since he was always running in multiple directions, teaching in both buildings and usually coaching something, and sometimes working a part-time mall job.

Mike Dewey sold insurance and investments in Pinicon, was active in church, and chaired the parks and recreation commission. Seated in Joe's office, he said he wanted to share a project from his daughter's tenth-grade health class. "I can't think of anything worse than a room full of sophomores in health class," he said, shaking his head.

"Some people would say that should qualify for hazard pay," Joe laughed. "And they're probably right!"

"Mr. Altman's health class sounds a whole lot better than what I had back in the day. They do some pretty hands-on and creative stuff, I think. But I want to show you this," he said, pulling out his cell phone. Joe flinched as Dewey showed a picture of students in Altman's health class putting a condom on a banana.

"I'm not trying to play gotcha, Joe. I'm really not. But seriously? I can't believe this got the OK with a bunch of sophomores."

Joe was speechless. "Uh, wow. If you're asking me if I knew this, no. I didn't."

"So I'm the first to come to you about this?" he asked.

"That you are, Mike. I appreciate it. Let me talk to Mr. Altman and get back to you."

"I hate to be the one to raise it. It seems a little much, though," he said, again almost apologetically as he closed the pictures on his phone.

"I'd like to have the pictures, if you don't mind," Joe said as they walked toward the office door. "Give me a little time and I'll be in touch, OK?"

Dewey was scarcely out of Joe's office when Joyce Barry walked in, with wide eyes. "Are you aware of Mr. Altman's health project?" she asked awkwardly.

"I am now."

"This is completely inappropriate and an embarrassment to the district if you want to know the truth. Talk about wrong messages! I bet the parents who didn't sign their kids out of the class would have if they would have known this was coming. I think we need to . . ."

Joe cut her off. "Curriculum can be controversial, can't it, Joyce? Kind of like deciding how much web content to filter here at school. If you'll excuse me, I have to get out into the building."

Joe often tried to disguise his many trips around the building as best he could. For example, if he was checking to see how two kids who were formerly fighting were getting along, he might come through their PE locker room, pretending to inventory padlocks or check the emergency lights. Or he might just discretely pull up next to a student in English and ask for an explanation of what she was studying. The main objective was always the same—visibility. The secondary objective, however, was a close second—reconnaissance. "You can't be situationally aware if you're holed up in your office," Summers had warned. Based on Jeralyn's concern that the building was suffering from climate challenges, Joe's reconnaissance and situational awareness needed to improve.

He was halfway to the auto shop when his cell phone rang. Dr. Zylstra. *Perfect*, he thought sarcastically. He wondered if Altman's banana lesson was the reason for her call. "Good morning, Carol. How are you?"

"Fine, Joe. Say, what do you know about a condom lesson in Altman's health class?"

"I know that word travels fast. I just had a parent share pictures with me. I have to think he captured students' attention," he said, wondering how she would take his attempt at levity.

"It may be a slow news day, but I've got a reporter coming over. Apparently Mr. Altman had kids do the same project at Kessler High."

Joe said he was on his way to meet Altman, who should be returning from driver's education about then. "I'll call you right back."

Joe had asked custodian Dave Crawford to designate a parking spot for the driver's ed car next to the building to help Altman rush between classes. As Altman pulled in, Joe slid into the driver's seat of the car. "Nothing like a little winter driver's ed to get the heart pumping," Altman laughed. "I'm actually glad to have some slick streets," he said. "A lot of their parents won't let them drive in the snow. They need the practice."

Joe agreed and said he hoped Altman and Elliott would make it through the class unscathed. Joe then asked about the health unit.

"It's going great. The Empowering Educators Conference had great ideas for making the class more relevant. The kids have seen it as a blow-off in the past, so I'm trying to bring it to life a little. Much more hands-on."

"Right," Joe said. "I've talked to a few folks in the last hour about the anatomy part. Specifically the condom lesson with the banana."

"Yeah. Most of them showed really good maturity on the reproduction stuff. Very few parents signed their kids out, too. We're sure not doing worksheets anymore!"

Joe explained that Zylstra had called and was getting ready for a media interview about the lesson. "We've got parents in both schools who are pretty upset." Altman asked if Joe was uncomfortable with the assignment.

"I know I'm uncomfortable with the media getting a hold of it. Parents I can handle, but this is not going to play well," Joe said. "Step back and think about the perception."

Altman could see Joe's wheels turning. "Joe, I'm sorry if I've created a problem. This hands-on stuff has worked great for all the other units. I didn't see a problem with this, especially since I spent so much time in the setup. I told them they would be graded over the way they handled it in terms of maturity. They were probably more off task when we did matching worksheets and labeling things with the projector. We did clay models of the heart and other organs, and that went great. In fact, I was gonna see if you could get us into the virtual reality cave at the community college for some models of the heart. Anyway, I thought clay was a little too much for the reproductive unit, so I chose this instead. It all came from the Empowering Educators Conference, and they said they had great results."

"There's no doubt that hands-on is more engaging and, honestly, probably a better way. But this is *way* too hands-on for a lot of folks. Do me a favor and give me a copy of all your stuff for the lesson. Plans, objectives, setup, notes, alignment with the curriculum, stuff from the conference, OK? ASAP."

Altman apologized again and promised to get Joe the notes as soon as he returned from Kessler High. In his return call to Zylstra, Joe said Altman had been working hard to make the health class more rigorous using things he had brought back from the Empowering Educators Conference. "They did clay models with other body systems, which of course makes sense, but he thought clay was a bad idea for this topic."

"So he had kids put *condoms on bananas*?" Zylstra snapped.

"Said he had less messing around than in other years," Joe said.

"Well, that's not the case at Kessler High," she said. "You better talk to Murphy. What's the deal with this guy?"

Joe repeated that Altman was a strong teacher who was working hard to bring the health class alive, but acknowledged that he may have blown it in terms of parental reactions. Regardless of the wisdom of Altman's judgment, Joe felt obligated to defend him because of the energy and hard work he brought to both Pinicon and Kessler. Zylstra interrupted and said she would call Joe right back.

Joe sat for a minute, mind racing. *How does a guy decide that clay genital models are too controversial but putting a condom on a banana is OK? Practically speaking, how do you handle the topic appropriately and in a way that actually teaches something? Do students rise to the level of expectations placed upon them? What if Altman was right and that there had been less messing around with this lesson than the old worksheets? Am I too naïve? What will people say about how much the conference cost? And this is what they brought back?*

Joe's phone chirped, interrupting his questions. Zylstra again. "Joe, Don Mitchell just talked to Altman. We're putting him on administrative reassignment for a couple of days, mostly for PR's sake. The television people up here are going crazy, and Don is making the statement. If anyone contacts you, refer any media to him."

So much for defending Altman, Joe thought, looking out the window at the empty driver's ed parking spot. *It must have been a short conversation with Mitchell.* Joe asked Carrie for Altman's mobile number, but Carrie couldn't find it. "Apparently he has changed his number or something," she said.

"That can't happen! We've got a teacher and kids in a driver's ed car and we can't get a hold of them? That's not OK. We've got to have a better process."

Immediately, Joe knew how his words came across to Carrie, who had turned away to busy herself with something on her desk.

"Carrie, I'm sorry. I'm not blaming you. I shouldn't have said it that way."

"It's fine. We should have the number. I guess it fell through the cracks," she said, trying to sound normal, despite the fact that her neck was flushed red.

"Again, I'm sorry. I'll talk to Gregg."

His phone chirped again. Claire.

"What's up?" he asked.

"Hi, hon; how's your day?"

"It was fine until about an hour ago. What do you need?" he asked, more tersely than intended.

"Nothing. Just wanted to see how you are. Margaret wanted Subway and I thought we could all go since there's no game tonight, but we can talk about it later."

"I'm sorry. Just bad timing on a couple of things here. . . ."

"It's fine. I'll talk to you later. Or I'll take the kids. Bye."

Joe felt like he was being peppered from all sides, mishandling most of it and taking it out on two of the people who contributed most to any of his success—his secretary and his wife. He needed some fresh air and a stroll through the student parking lot. He was angry with himself, with Altman, with Mitchell, with the media. He welcomed the sting of the February wind.

REMEMBER YOUR OFFER?

Joe had made it a point to speak with Jerome Hayes, Javaris's father, any time he could. Since the Hayes family regularly attended just about every Pinicon event, it had not been hard to do, though their conversations were usually small talk. While he was careful not to assume that Jerome Hayes spoke for anyone but himself and his own family, Joe decided to accept the invitation Hayes had given the previous August, when he said Joe was welcome to contact him if he had any concerns or issues with the African-American Kessler transfer students.

"I appreciate that you're reaching out, Mr. Gentry. It's a pleasure to talk with you."

Joe explained that he and Jeralyn were always trying to monitor Pinicon's culture and climate and that they were interested in Hayes's impressions a few months in to the school year.

"As I told you last fall, Javaris struggled in Atlanta. He never really fit in. Things were better at Kessler, but he still felt like an outsider. Pinicon has certainly been better in that sense," the senior Hayes explained.

"Have you heard Javaris, any of the other Kessler transfer kids, or their families talk about difficulties here? Have they talked about feeling like outsiders or being poorly treated? I'm asking about the whole spectrum, from being the new kid to being treated poorly or harassed on racial lines."

"Well, you're leaving it wide open, aren't you?" Hayes laughed. "Honestly, I haven't heard a lot. Now, there have been a few things here and there with those Confederate flags and a few comments, but that's not surprising."

"We've tried to deal with the flag issue, and any name-calling or harassment is unacceptable. We're committed to making Pinicon feel like home for every kid. Of course I know that will take some time, but I also know we have to be intentional about it and not expect good things to happen by themselves," Joe said.

"I appreciate that. I think the negatives are pretty subtle and probably imperceptible to many, except perhaps to our folks of color or those who are really watching. You know, in today's America, we often say we're post-racial or beyond some of the divisive issues of the past. And in some ways that's true. But it's also an easy thing to *say* if we've never had to actually *demonstrate it*. Folks I talk to don't feel overt hostility as much as a lack of awareness."

"And who lacks the awareness . . .?"

"Not everyone, of course, but some teachers, kids, the community," Hayes said.

Joe thanked him for his time and insight and said he was collecting additional information before making a plan to move forward to address the concerns. "I want you to know that I'm open to your ideas and suggestions as we work on this. I hope you'll feel comfortable sharing information or suggestions. The door's open. Don't wait for me to call."

"Oh, I surely won't," Hayes said.

Two days later, a copy of *Why Are All the Black Kids Sitting Together in the Cafeteria?* arrived in Joe's mailbox with a note from Hayes. *I'm sure you have a long reading list, but this might be a starting point for your thought process. Regards, Jerome L. Hayes.*

WHEN AND HOW TO SUPPORT?

"Costa Rica was fabulous!" Professor Summers announced over the phone. "We'd definitely go back. We're in Houston now. Our flight to Key West has been delayed, so I thought I'd check in."

The call was a welcomed surprise on a day when Joe felt like the gray winter was having its way with him. He told Professor Summers about recent events, including the banana lesson controversy.

Joe said Altman had been working hard to strengthen the health class and implement ideas from the Empowering Educators Conference, but acknowledged that Altman should have anticipated objections to the bananas. "But in his defense, if it's good for teaching the lungs or brain, should he go back to worksheets for the reproductive system? I know it's probably too hot to handle for sophomores, but it's about appropriate information."

"You said the key word. Appropriate. Don Mitchell likes getting on TV, but he won't enjoy this one," Summers said. "Some teachers might do this to make a scene, but if this guy is good, the best you can do is support him, even if it is behind the scenes. Tell him just what you told me and that in the future you want him to run things like this past you first. Sounds like his heart is in the right place. He just didn't think it through."

"We've got a good teacher trying to do good work. Maybe his judgment wasn't great, but he gets suspended? I don't know," Joe vented.

"A learning experience for everyone," Summers advised.

Joe also shared the story about Heidi Morris's breast pumping and the visit from Diane Watters. "I had no idea how much of my time would be spent somewhere between a social worker and counselor. I'm amazed at some of the things people bring to me!"

The professor laughed and said, "I've got a lifetime of stories, but none quite like that. The conference principals' response to the racial stuff at the Piedmont game is also disappointing, but keep pushing and build a power base with Judy Christensen from Fox Valley and the others who get it. You're going to have to help the others see it."

Joe agreed. "Raising the issue is definitely the right thing to do, but there are a few people here who think I favor the Kessler kids. Jeez. Even I said it. I hate it when people say *Kessler kids*. I mean the *transfer kids* from Kessler, some of them black. I'm trying to make everyone *our kids*, but some think I'm handing out special treatment."

"You can't control others' perceptions. You can control what you do in the best interest of every kid, and it sounds like you're trying. Now, when was the last time you did something fun with your family? How's Elliott?"

Joe said his family had enjoyed a relaxing break and that he, Sutt, and Kristi also managed to get together. "Tom McHale pretty much forced us to make the time and I'm glad he did. As for Elliott, I think he's doing OK. He's a quiet kid. Basketball is going alright."

Professor Summers suggested Joe find some ways to get uninterrupted one-on-one time with Elliott to really get at how things were going. "Our kids would open up and talk if I could get them in the car on the way to somewhere. Just remember that there's always more going on than meets the eye."

They ended their conversation with Professor Summers advising Joe to revisit the message he shared with the teachers back in August. "See how you think you're doing with that. Late winter can be tough on everybody. Keep up the positive energy. And get some time with your family. No shop talk."

"I know, I know. Good advice. I really appreciate the call. This was a fun surprise."

"Hey, one last thing. What are you reading right now?"

"You got me there. Mostly that God-awful state testing manual, yearly progress, new requirements from the feds. Really fun stuff," he said sarcastically.

"That doesn't count. I want you reading something professionally, for twenty minutes a day, uninterrupted. No exceptions. And something for pleasure on your own. Doesn't matter what it is, a mystery, something escapist. You've gotta unplug that brain a little. Let me know what you choose."

Chapter 3
THE PEOPLE'S BUSINESS

Joe and Murphy agreed that the best way to ensure Don Mitchell's support of an idea was to get Dr. Zylstra excited about it first. They accomplished just that when they proposed inviting area legislators to spend the day in their respective schools. "It's such an obvious thing to do, but it doesn't happen near enough," she said.

Faculty meetings in both buildings had to be rescheduled in order to align the invitation with the designated constituent days when the legislators were available. State Representative Mike Hansen enthusiastically accepted Joe's invitation. "My sister's a teacher and I know how hard she works. I'll plan to be there first thing in the morning," he said.

True to his word, Representative Hansen arrived in Joe's office shortly after 7:15 a.m., escorted by the Pinicon Pal who had been assigned as his host. He shadowed the Pal in the morning and sat in on a variety of classes in the afternoon. Immediately after school, Rhonda Prior met him before the faculty meeting, at which subcommittees would report their work on defining the Pinicon Way.

Joe had hoped to spend more time with Hansen, but as was often the case, the day played out otherwise. There were, thankfully, no big crises or discipline problems during the visit, just the usual harried lives of principals and teachers.

"I've got to tell you, I'm exhausted," Hansen said at the end of the faculty meeting. "I'm used to eating quickly when the legislature's in session, but that was fast. And I'll tell you what else. The girl I shadowed this morning is doing some neat stuff. That advertising project in English was amazing, and what a great thing for kids to start learning about the stock market in Econ. Some of their stocks were doing pretty well!"

Joe reiterated that the goal was not to put on a show but rather to portray an average day. He handed Hansen a copy of the major things that were under way at Pinicon, including the sharing arrangement with Kessler, implementing ideas from the Empowering Educators Conference, TeachShare, Saturday School, and the subcommittee work on defining the Pinicon Way.

"What are the main things you want me to take from this experience?" Hansen asked.

Joe seized, hearing precisely the question he had hoped for. "That contrary to what you may hear in the media about test scores and terrible teachers, there are some great things happening here. We're a long way from perfect, but we're actively building on the good stuff to *get better*. Hopefully, you saw that all day and in our faculty meeting. What's the main thing that stands out to you?"

"That they're doing so much more than when I was in school. There's just no comparison," Hansen answered quickly.

They talked for another hour, touching on everything from high school sports, to Pinicon's need for updated technology and tech support, to the challenges of being a first-year principal and ways it might be similar to managing a trucking company, which was Hansen's real job, in addition to being a legislator. Before leaving, Hansen asked what Joe thought are the best ways to measure teacher and school quality.

Joe jumped again. "Everyone's obsessed with test scores, or so it seems. At least the media and legislators," he said with a smile. "But that's really only one piece of the puzzle. And most people have no idea what's on those tests, yet test scores get held up as some kind of Holy Grail."

"I never did too well on those tests," Hansen confided.

"Exactly. And they've increased ten times," Joe added. "I read about a businessman who's on a school board somewhere. He took the state achievement tests and publicized his score as a way to start a discussion about the tests and what they show. At times, I'd like to try the same thing."

Joe could see Hansen's wheels turning. "That's a hell of an idea. Let's think about that."

Hansen said he planned to challenge his colleagues to request visits to schools, rather than waiting for invitations. He also said he planned to subscribe to Joe's blog and asked him to keep in touch as the legislative session moved forward. Though it was one more thing added to his list, Joe promised to do so as he walked Hansen to his car.

HUNG OUT?

Thirty minutes later, Joe caught Altman on the phone.

"Do you have a few minutes?" Joe asked.

"Sure. I need a break from my home improvement projects. You know, trying to use my suspension time wisely," Altman said. "I have to tell you, though, that the last several calls I've had from Kessler and Pinicon administration haven't been positive. This one makes me a little nervous."

"I hate the timing of this conversation, Gregg, but that can't be helped," Joe said. "You know I'd rather talk in person, but I need to ask about the trip to the airport for the Empowering Educators Conference."

Altman told essentially the same story that Watters had shared.

"Boy, you're right, Joe. Your timing sucks. I'm not sure the district means what it says about engaging students and improving instruction. I tried that and got myself suspended or whatever they call this. Not to mention a lecture from Don Mitchell that was unlike anything I've had since junior high," he complained. "I feel like I was hung out to dry. Like you guys want all this new stuff until there's a little flak, and then we go back to the status quo. I'd be seen as a better teacher if I were passing out matching worksheets and letting the kids do homework for the last ten minutes of class! And I would have stayed out of the news. And now you're asking whether Heidi is some kind of hose bag."

Joe said he felt bad about the suspension and that he had been unable to reach him while Zylstra and Mitchell were moving quickly. "I want you to know, Gregg, that I told them both what a good teacher you are and that you've really worked hard on new ideas from the conference. And the thing with Heidi is a dead issue as far as I'm concerned."

Joe said the clay models were a great way to teach anatomy, but that there were limits. "You made a good decision to not do clay models for the reproductive unit. You avoided that curricular landmine, but I let you step on another. I need to help you anticipate those. Part of that is on me."

In accepting some of the blame, Joe was harkening back to a lesson he learned as a young coach. Sometimes the leader has to take more of the blame than is deserved. He sometimes told his teams that the blame for a tough loss rested with him for not having them better prepared. He hoped it took some of the sting out of Altman's suspension, the letters to the editor, and damage to his reputation.

He wasn't sure if Altman felt any better. He spent the next ninety minutes working through several drafts of his blog and newspaper column before settling on a version that he felt captured his feelings on the issue, without specifically mentioning Altman by name.

IT'S YOUR SCHOOL

Although he had intended to meet regularly with the student council, it had been a couple of months since Joe had found the time. He wondered if that was poor time management on his part or the reality of a murderous schedule. Whatever the case, he felt he had a good rapport with the student members, who seemed receptive to the message he always gave when he was able to meet with them. *This is your school and you're its leaders. Take that opportunity.*

Joe had thought a lot about his conversations with the Pinicon Pals, Kessler transfers, and parents regarding the building's culture and climate. It came to him one day that, while the leadership team and faculty subcommittees were spending a lot of time defining the Pinicon Way, he had not asked the same of the students. *If it really is their school, they ought to be doing the same work*, he thought.

After he explained his request to the council, a few hands shot up. Rhonda Prior's son, Ben, spoke first. "I've heard my mom talking about the Pinicon Way stuff that the teachers are working on, and it's cool that you asked us to work on it too."

This prompted a lot of discussion. As Joe passed out a handout he had adapted from one given to teachers months before, it was clear that some students understood what Joe wanted better than others. But it seemed that the majority understood, were intrigued by the idea, or both. Joe told them he would like to observe some of their meetings, but that he did not intend to dictate their work or the outcomes. "You've heard me say this is *your school* and I mean that. This is your opportunity to define what it means to be students here and how we do things. I want you all to *own* that."

He sat quietly at the back of the room and observed the remainder of their meeting, reminding himself how important it was for principals to, as McHale often said, "seek out the good stuff." Spending some time with student leaders, away from breast pumps, bananas, mind-numbing testing manuals, and ethnic tension was just what he needed. *Man, we've got some good kids,* he said to himself.

QUESTIONS

1. Evaluate Joe's latest interaction with Don Mitchell.
2. Evaluate Joe's handling of Gregg Altman's banana lesson. How much support from the principal should Altman receive from Joe?
3. How effective was State Representative Mike Hansen's visit to Pinicon? What ideas do you have for effectively engaging legislators? How should Joe proceed?

Chapter Four

Late February

Data, Evidence, and Unpredictability

YOU'RE NOT GOING TO GET ANYWHERE

Oliver Ortiz was a small, quiet boy who was easy to miss, particularly because he skipped school so frequently. He would be absent for a couple days, return and become frustrated by how far behind he was, and leave school in the middle of the day. It wasn't unusual for a retired woman who lived across the street to call and ask to speak to Joe about everything from the way the school lawn was mowed, to classroom lights that were left on at night, to students' driving habits, but her favorite seemed to be calling to report seeing a truant Oliver leaving school.

A few times, Joe had jumped in Young's Camaro, located Oliver, and brought him back. Olver's father, Karl, worked on and off at the Trailways Lounge. When he needed to speak with him, Joe tried to make his calls in the late morning. Conversations on days when Joe called too late had not gone well.

Joe saw Oliver as an example of how student discipline cases needed to be handled with flexibility. According to the Pinicon handbook, students leaving school without permission were to be suspended. Excessive unexcused absences could warrant a call to the county attorney and truancy charges, though the Pinicon county attorney had shown no interest. Carrie and Jeralyn both said Oliver's case had to be handled carefully. "Karl's fine, but he's gone a lot. Oliver's stepbrother is bad news and I'd hate to see him knocking little Oliver around," Jeralyn said. It was 11:47 a.m. when Joe called Karl to tell him Oliver had refused to return to school. He usually cringed if the phone rang more than four or five times before Karl answered or voicemail kicked on. Today, it was pushing twelve rings and voicemail was full, so he hung up.

"Carrie, I'm going down to the Trailways to see Karl Ortiz. I know he's not answering because he recognizes the number. Would you ask Jeralyn to cover me in the cafeteria, please?"

"Sure . . . ," Carrie said with a confused look on her face.

The dimly lit Trailways Lounge had a sticky film on the floor, though it wasn't as rough looking as Joe had anticipated. The place was nearly empty as Joe walked toward the bar.

"You got a lunch special today?" he asked Karl as he eased onto a barstool.

"Right there on the board," he gestured with his back turned, unaware that Joe was his customer.

"I'll take the ham and cheese," Joe said.

"And to drink?" Karl asked, turning around and seeing Joe for the first time. He paused, lips pursed. "Well, this is a little different." Karl, unlike his son, stood maybe six feet, five inches, with gray eyes and a bodybuilder's physique.

"I thought it might work better to catch you here face-to-face. Maybe less of an interruption than talking on the phone," Joe said. "And I've never been here before."

"Don't get many from school in here," he snorted.

"Oliver left Mrs. Prior's geometry class again. I found him walking but he wouldn't come back. This is his fourth unexcused absence this quarter. That's going to cause him to be suspended. I don't want to mess with the county attorney and truancy charges, and I know you're tired of getting my calls. I want him in school, but what we're doing isn't working."

Karl had a habit of trying to finish people's sentences. And he had become pretty good at finishing Joe's, since the reasons for their communication were always the same: Oliver skipping school and failing.

"I don't know what you want me to do. Be right with you guys," he said to two men from a construction crew who shuffled in. "We've been around and around with that school for years. Nothing ever changes. He comes, he skips, you call, I'm pissed, he flunks."

"I know it seems like an endless cycle. I'm not sure what to do either, so I chase after him and try to bring him back."

Karl's tone switched. "The fact is, it's always something with that damn school. Every time he does something good, you guys find a way to fuck it up. If it isn't a teacher, it's some bullshit rule. Here's the bottom line. You're never going to get anywhere with my son, 'cause he thinks you're a real asshole."

Before he knew what had come out of his mouth, Joe heard himself say, "Well, Karl, a lot of people up there who agree with your son."

Karl paused. Snickered. Sighed. "I suppose there are," he said, sliding his ham and cheese in front of him.

"Karl, I want to help, but we can't do that if he's not at school. We're trying, but there are limits to what we can do. I'd like to talk about it and find a way to turn this around."

"I been trying for seventeen years," Karl said, walking away. "You boys know what you want?" he hollered to the construction workers.

WE'VE GOT A PROBLEM DOWN HERE

Joe had just typed out an e-mail to Professor Summers about the professional book he had chosen to read—Lencioni's (2002) *The Five Dysfunctions of a Team*—when his radio chirped. "Joe, we need you in the cafeteria study hall right now. Mrs. Watters and Heidi Morris are getting into it!" he heard Dave Crawford say. Joe's heart jumped, his memory flashing instantly back to Bill Kurowski's accident. *Just like Facebook and the bleachers, nothing good ever comes over the two-way radio,* he thought as he ran down the hall.

He could hear shouting before he rounded the corner. Heidi Morris was standing in a classroom doorway facing Diane Watters, who was shaking her finger at Heidi. "I know about your little stunt and it better not happen again, you little slut," Diane hissed.

Joe looked at Petersen, who stood frozen at the study hall desk with wide eyes. Joe motioned for him to take the students down the hall toward the gym. He didn't want them seeing any more of the show than they already had. Petersen ambled toward Joe with a confused look on his face and asked, "Is there something you want me to do?"

"I want you to get the students out of here. Take them to the gym. Now."

"You have no business coming here and disrupting my class," Heidi said.

"You have no business disrupting my marriage, you little whore!" Diane shrieked, prompting a loud, "Whoa! Cat fight!" from several study hall boys. Petersen's study hall was exiting much more slowly than Joe would have liked.

Joe squeezed himself into the space between the two women. "Ladies, this is not the time or place. Diane, you need to leave. Heidi, why don't you take a few minutes in the lounge or my office? We'll take care of your class."

Morris seemed amenable to Joe's instructions, but Diane remained firmly in her path at the door. "Diane. Now. Move," Joe said, taking her by the elbow. "Carrie, Ms. Morris is coming up to my office; would you please have Jeralyn meet her there right now? And we need to cover her class," Joe called into the radio.

Diane Watters ripped her elbow from Joe's grasp and started down the hall. Joe followed her, trying not to agitate her further. Diane, you can't do this. I know you're upset, but you've disrupted the whole school and made things worse for everybody. It's not acceptable."

"I'm not going to stand around and watch that bitch unravel my marriage. That's unacceptable! Did you notice how she didn't deny it? Sexual predators have no business around kids," she growled, prompting students and a few teachers to peer out of their classroom doors.

Just then Mark Watters appeared behind them. "Diane! What the hell's going on?" She refused to turn around and smacked the crash bar on the exterior door hard. Joe looked at Watters, who stood in the hallway, stunned. "I think you better go with her, Mark. We'll cover your class. Just go."

Joe felt paralyzed as he watched the confrontation between husband and wife on the front sidewalk. When he noticed students watching from classroom windows, he walked outside. "I have to ask you both to leave school. You can't stay here. This is disruptive. Both of you, please leave, now," Joe said, a little more firmly than he intended.

"Damn it, Joe, can you give us a minute? This is private!"

"Mark, I know, but it's not private *here*. The kids are watching. You have to go."

Watters looked up and saw faces watching the conflict through the windows. He did his best to collect himself and followed his wife toward the parking lot. Joe motioned for the students watching from the windows to get back to class. *Why are teachers letting them watch?* He did a quick rundown of the associates or substitutes he might be able to get on a moment's notice. Joe could cover, but he thought he had done too much of that already. Plus, he was scheduled in a special ed meeting in fifteen minutes. He asked Carrie to start working on a sub for Watters's class right away.

Hearing the bell, he walked back past Morris's room and saw that she was back at her desk. He slipped in and asked if she was OK to continue the rest of the day. She said she was. "I'm not letting her get in the way of my work," she said, as if nothing had happened.

"Fair enough. We'll talk some more about this soon," Joe said.

He headed to the gym to tell Petersen to bring his study hall back. When he entered the gym, he saw a raucous scene. Students were on their feet chanting and yelling, with playground balls flying everywhere. Petersen was leaning against the bleachers in the far side of the gym.

"It's the dodgeball championship, Mr. Gentry! Wanna join in?" a junior boy asked.

Joe smiled and declined.

"You can take your kids back to study hall, Stu," he said.

Joe shook his head as he left the gym. *Dodgeball and championship.* Only *Stu Petersen*, he thought. *What a day.*

INVITATION ACCEPTED

"We're coming up on the twenties in American History. If your offer to team teach is still on the table, maybe we ought to talk about it," Pat Patrazzo said, as he sorted through his mail in the outer office.

"I'd love to, Pat." Joe responded, looking up from his cell phone. "What do you have in mind?"

"I'm not a good one to ask. Altman, Watters, and the others came back from that conference pretty excited. I figured it might be a good way to try some of their ideas. I hate the twenties anyway, so maybe you can help."

Unable to conceal his excitement, Joe said he could rearrange his schedule that afternoon to meet Patrazzo during his planning time to talk about ideas. Though Patrazzo didn't show the same enthusiasm, the two had a productive conversation in which Joe asked what Patrazzo thought were his best and least effective lessons in the twenties unit.

"I always felt like I did my best when I matched the curriculum to teaching in a way that was fun for *me*," he told Patrazzo.

"To be honest, the textbook is pretty much the curriculum in here," Patrazzo confided. "But I'm a lot better with the early stuff, like pre-Civil War."

After comparing ideas, they settled on giving the kids a survey and pretest about things they knew or thought they knew related to the twenties.

"I'll throw together some ideas for the survey in a Google Doc and have you take a look. How about if you add or delete anything you want? When we get the results back, let's take a look at the curriculum guide and see what we've got. Maybe we'll use the textbook and maybe we won't. Sound OK?" Joe asked.

He was surprised when Patrazzo confided that he didn't know how to access the Google document.

"OK, well, that's not a big deal. I would show you right now, but I'm gonna be late for a conference call in a couple minutes. We could set up a time later this week. The other option would be for me to send a student aide up to show you. There should be a couple in the office now."

Joe smiled when he left, feeling as though he had taken a major step forward with Patrazzo. He made up the story about the conference call, hoping Patrazzo would accept some help from a student. Just a few weeks before, he would have never expected that Patrazzo would accept his offer to explore some team teaching opportunities. Joe wondered what accounted for the apparent change of heart. Whatever it was, it felt like a new start to a relationship that needed it. *I'm not going to screw it up this time*, he said to himself.

Chapter 4

LUNCH MONITOR

"Joe, Don Mitchell's on line two for you," Carrie said.

Joe put his feet up on the desk, still high from the apparent progress with Patrazzo. "Hey, Don. I just had a great conversation with Pat Patrazzo about some team teaching we're gonna try. I bet you didn't see that coming. How's *your* day?"

"Patrazzo, huh? Well, my day will be better once I know what you were doing at the Trailways for lunch Tuesday."

Mitchell's words felt like a cold, wet blanket and Joe felt himself deflate. He reached for the lucky buckeye in his pocket as he stretched out his legs. *Be professional but don't take any bullshit,* Joe told himself. *Zylstra will think going to meet Karl Ortiz off school grounds is great. Who cares if Mitchell doesn't?*

Before Joe thought about it, he said, "They've got a helluva ham and cheese lunch special, Don. You ought to come down. I'll buy."

Mitchell hesitated. "Yeah, funny. So what is going on?"

"We've got a boy with a lot of truancy issues. Dad works there . . . tough situation. I try to catch him at the right times, but he stopped taking my calls. So I tried to see him in person to mix it up a little. Maybe I can establish a little rapport by meeting on his turf. We'll see." Joe paused. "Why do you ask?"

"Had a couple calls about people seeing you down there during the day."

"Is that a problem? I'm not hitting happy hour. I've met with a few parents off campus."

Mitchell seemed off-balance and hesitated again. Joe felt good that he, not Mitchell, was controlling the conversation for once. "No, no problem really. Just a little weird. You know how people watch things."

"Yeah, well to be honest, this dad is a little different, so maybe this will help. I'll keep you posted," Joe said, knowing full well that Mitchell wasn't interested in any updates on his progress with Karl Ortiz unless it meant fewer calls coming into the Kessler Central Office. Joe was resisting the temptation to speculate on who might have made the call. *Pointless,* he told himself.

"Well, just remember that you're living in the fishbowl and everyone sees everything you do," Mitchell cautioned. "It's a perception thing."

"Understood. I hope what they're seeing is a school that's trying to make an effort to help a student and family experience some success in school. Thanks for the heads up, Don. And I'm serious about the lunch special."

SO MUCH DATA, SO LITTLE INFORMATION

Joe had been concerned that he might be throwing too much at Pinicon teachers at once. With few exceptions, faculty meetings had felt productive, at least from his perspective, and teachers had become accustomed to using time together for issues related to teaching and learning and getting mundane details via Joe's blog. The leadership team assured him that efforts to infuse ideas from the Empowering Educators Conference were well received. Joe agreed, having seen evidence of some new practices during classroom observations. The leadership team also said subcommittees working on aspects of defining the Pinicon Way were making steady progress and engaged in some lively discussions. Increasing teachers' use of TeachShare was another priority, and it seemed to be catching on among some.

Joe continued to try and utilize big questions at the start of meetings. The problem with this approach was that teachers often wanted to debate the question so long that little time was left for the actual agenda. He tried to strike a balance while remembering that teachers had thanked him in December for the opportunity to wrangle with big, philosophical issues in education.

"I'm trying to strike a balance between endless debate and practical things that can help us immediately," he said at the start of the faculty meeting. "Some of you have seen my eyes glazed over from the state testing manual and all the reports we have to file, but it reminds me of something very important—the amount of information we have access to about our students' progress. There's actually more than we may find useful, but if we don't use some of it, we're missing an opportunity."

Joe then explained that, in addition to the other initiatives that teachers were working on, he wanted to start exploring Pinicon students' performance on state tests. "A few ground rules. First, know that this is *the start* of an exploration. I've asked several of you informally about how test scores and state reports have been used in the past. The consistent answer seems to be *not much*. And that's nobody's fault. A lot of schools are in the same place. Second, know that I prefer the word *evidence* over the word *data*. I think we use *data* too much and it implies that scores and percentages are all that matter. We know that's garbage. Numbers are fine, but they're not the only thing."

As he spoke, Joe felt similar to the way he did during the opening meeting with teachers the previous August. Back then, the goal had been to make a good first impression. The issue was no longer one of first impressions. Instead, he hoped that teachers would feel comfortable starting to look at test scores and other evidence of Pinicon students' progress, but not feel overwhelmed because they had never done so and he was simultaneously pushing them in other areas. *I may be overemphasizing that this is the start of an exploration, but better that than to freak them out with one more thing on top of what we're already doing,* he thought to himself.

He explained that the leadership team had developed some options for teachers to begin the exploration he was talking about. The first was for teachers to actually take certain tests. Another was to examine, in cross-curricular teams, scores from the last several years. A third was to compare, in teams, the content of the tests with the content and timing of Pinicon courses.

"With Mrs. Morris covering classes while you observe one another, I hope this will be a challenging process that informs us about our teaching and curriculum, but one that's also fun and that plays into defining the Pinicon Way," he said. "With the rest of the time today, I want you to form small groups to react, ask questions, and consider which option appeals to you most."

Joe spent the rest of the meeting circulating and listening to conversations. As was typical, Prior and a few others lingered after the meeting officially ended, still talking.

"I know you're worried that we might be taking on too much," Prior said. "And we might be, but when some of these things have gone so long without any attention, we have to start somewhere."

Martinson nodded. "We've done data walls and pretty bulletin boards with all kinds of charts in the past, but not much else. This will take a while, but I think it's worth doing."

"Do you think it's too much at once, because I'm worried about that. Even after the leadership team said we should go ahead with this today, I hesitated. In fact, I almost punted on the whole thing and canceled the meeting today to give people some extra work time," Joe said.

"It's a lot at once," Den Herder said. "But Rhonda's right. You gotta start sometime. And if it's too much, we can back off. The good thing about it is that some people who haven't been as engaged with other things might really dig into this. And it's good that we can choose how we want to be involved."

"That was Watters and the leadership team's idea," Joe said.

He left the meeting still feeling cautious and hesitant, but affirmed by the conversation with those who stayed late. He told McHale on the phone that he was cautiously optimistic.

SKYPE CONFERENCE

When Joe told Kristi about Mitchell calling to ask why he had been at Trailways Lounge, they were split on how he came across to Mitchell.

"That Mitchell guy sounds hard to read," Sutt said. "One minute, he's gruff and sour, but he praised the hell out of you at the board meeting on the Saturday School thing."

"Like you said, Joe, you know Dr. Zylstra will love what you're trying to do and she's his boss, so who cares?" Kristi asked.

"I probably was a little bit snippy, but I was also half serious. If Mitchell would get out of that office a little and get in touch with those of us in the trenches, it would help our morale and his credibility at the same time. Not gonna happen, though."

"Joe, I blogged about that legislator who came to visit Pinicon and how you guys talked about getting real people to take the state tests. My superintendent says I need to tone it down, though," Kristi complained.

"Seriously? Why?" Sutt asked.

"Says it comes across way too snarky, especially from a first-year principal. Says it has probably already damaged the district's relationship with the department of ed and the state superintendent of education."

"What a wuss. I read it and wouldn't change a thing," Sutt said.

"Kristi, I have to agree. You haven't said anything unprofessional. You've asked all the right questions. At least someone is paying attention for once. What is the harm in that? Is your super just a good ol' boy or what?" Joe asked.

Kristi said the superintendent felt the tone of her blog was aggressive and disrespectful. "He didn't like that I suggested maybe the governor should be removed from office if unemployment and crime don't fall during his term, since he wants to make it easier to fire teachers of low scoring students."

"Damn straight," Sutt barked.

"There must be something going on. Does the district have a site visit or some kind of appeal case with the state?" Joe asked.

Kristi knew of no problems with the department of ed and said she hesitated to tone down her opinions in the blog. "I added a disclaimer to the blog and my profile that says all the opinions are my own. Nowhere does it say I am the principal at Winthrop Elementary. And I actually had a few teachers and parents say they liked it. And a couple want to take the tests!"

Sutt suggested she be careful and avoid alienating the superintendent, but joined Joe in encouraging Kristi not to censor herself too much. "I think your super and Don Mitchell might be in the same league."

Joe spoke next. "Having our state rep here *was* great. Cal Murphy at Kessler High did the same thing. Funny your super is upset now, because I mentioned getting people to take the tests to the rep and he was interested. He said he did terrible on them when he was in school. Might be a way to start a conversation if we pushed it a little, but some people would be afraid of getting a bad score."

"Exactly," Sutt broke in. "And if those people are successful, what the hell does it say about some of the tests? It's the same thing I suggested to my conference principals last October. We're on to something."

FIELD TRIP

Roy Zimmerman, or "Sr." was the fifty-something-year-old father of Roy, better known as "Jr.," an eleventh grader whose IEP called for a couple of hours of resource assistance in special education. Rumor held that Sr., who had lived in Germany twenty years before, was worth millions from a massive inheritance. The two lived alone in a huge house on the edge of town, though Sr. was known to have many girlfriends.

One month Sr. would request an inordinate number of copies of IEPs and other documents. The next, it would be double copies of worksheets and homework assignments and an extra set of books so Sr. could be looking ahead at what teachers planned to teach in the next couple of weeks. He often sent e-mails that were several pages long and cc'd to special education administrators at the state department of education. Other times, he mailed handwritten letters directly to Joe, requesting schedule changes, a full-time associate for Jr., or that he be excused from homework for migraines, which Sr. described as "ungodly."

"Sr. is the classic case of a high-maintenance parent with nothing else to do but make everyone's life miserable, including his son, who is not a bad kid," Joe told the special ed problem-solving team in a private meeting. "Jr.'s biggest disability is his father, but we're all committed to working within the law and our responsibility. Having said that, our time is too valuable to waste on dad's nonsense. He's taking away from our ability to take care of our other kids, special needs and regular ed. If he wants to challenge us, that's his right."

Sr. had requested the meeting to review Jr.'s progress. After several previous meetings had spun in circles, Joe had vowed to set a firm agenda and time frame for all their meetings. He had learned that going above and beyond to cooperate only seemed to encourage Sr.'s impossible demands.

Sr. walked into the room, dressed in what appeared to be a new gray suit. He was accompanied by a grandmotherly-looking woman in her late sixties with salt-and-pepper, shoulder-length hair; and two young men who looked to be in their mid-twenties, dressed in sweatshirts. Five teachers were sitting in desks they had arranged in a semicircle.

"I don't believe we've met," Joe said, extending his hand to the woman. "I'm Joe Gentry, the principal."

"I'm Patricia Lynch, professor of education history at Wallace University. These are two of my students," she said gesturing toward the two young men. "We've been working with Mr. Zimmerman on his son's program."

"I see. Nice to meet you all," said Joe, caught off guard. "Roy, I didn't know you were bringing guests, or I would have arranged the room differently," he said, trying to ease the tension and also call attention to the surprise attack. He called Carrie and asked her to have some boys from study hall bring "three extra chairs for our guests."

"I prefer to be called *Senior*."

"I remember; sorry. We've allotted an hour for the meeting today and we're getting a bit of a late start. I want to thank the teachers for reworking their schedules to make themselves available. We have several teachers at home sick today, and we're short on substitute teachers, so we're especially short-handed." Sr. had settled into the one available chair while Lynch and the two students stood, waiting for the extra chairs.

"Jr. will be here pretty quick. He should be finishing up PE and is probably changing, Joe said, as he arranged the extra chairs tightly across the table from his teachers and gestured for the professor and students to take a seat.

"We won't need him for the meeting," Sr. said, pulling a note pad from a large black briefcase with *The Ultimate Driving Machine* embossed on it.

"Sr., as you had asked, Jr. and the teachers have worked on his weekly and monthly progress summary to share how things have been going. We think Jr. needs to be here to participate. His voice is pretty important here."

"I changed my mind. I don't want him here today. I'm the parent. I can do that, you know."

"You certainly can. I didn't realize you had changed your mind."

"Everyone here knows the situation. I've documented my conversations with Jr.," he said, flipping through the book. "I don't want him sitting here repeating what the teachers have told him to say."

Joe noticed that one of the law students had pulled a small video camera from his bag. "Sr., no one is telling him what to say. We're following his plan and working hard at it, as you can see by the number of teachers here. I didn't realize you were bringing guests and planning to record the meeting," Joe said, looking in the direction of the law student.

"The recording will help preserve an official record of our proceedings on behalf of my son, Roy Augustus Adler Zimmerman, Jr.," he said with great formality.

"I see. And I'd like to invite Professor Lynch to explain her role in the process." A hectic day, Sr.'s unpredictability, and the odd presence of a professor and college students had him feeling especially prickly.

"Professor Lynch is assisting me. I have that right," Sr. answered.

"Yes, Sr. Thank you. We'd like to hear from the professor."

Lynch explained her role at Wallace University, describing her interest in education history, one-room schoolhouses, phonics, violent video games, and the proliferation of youth sports. Joe loved that the professor had taken the bait and begun talking about herself. *Two can play this game, Sr.*, Joe thought, happily watching the minutes tick by as the pompous Lynch droned on, knowing Sr. was growing frustrated that he was not getting enough of the attention.

"Thank you, professor. I think we should hear from the teachers on Jr.'s progress since we met . . . ah . . . last month." Joe said.

Sr. interrupted. "I have several pages of sworn testimony from my son, and that is who we are here to talk about!" he shouted.

"I know, Sr., and thank you for that. You said you wanted more information than the weekly updates we're providing. These teachers who spend every day at school with Jr. have a lot to share."

Joe had promised the teachers that the meeting would last no more than one hour. "At sixty-one minutes, I am walking out the door, and you all are going in front of me. I promise." He had also told them that he wanted every bit of data on Jr.'s daily work, homework completion, test scores, interactions with peers, mood, etc. "I want scores, charts, anecdotes, stories, pictures, you name it." And the teachers delivered in volume.

One by one, each reported on Jr.'s progress in their classroom, citing the types of evidence Joe had suggested. Joe had compiled the reports into one document with charts and trend lines, all of which were tied to Jr.'s IEP. Some read their remarks, others spoke less formally, but all presented evidence that clearly demonstrated that the teachers were accommodating Jr.'s needs according to his IEP. Several of the teachers said their observations led them to believe that Jr. actually needed *less* support and assistance than the IEP currently called for.

During the teachers' overview, Carrie sent a text that Mrs. Hampton and Mrs. Barry had vomited and were headed home. Joe told her to send McCallister's student teacher to cover Hampton's class and ask Jeralyn to cover for Barry instead of coming to the meeting. That still left them short, but Carrie would figure it out.

After the teachers' presentation, Sr. rose to stand and asked if the camera was on. Reading from his legal pad, occasionally using German words, he rambled from reflections on the difficulty Jr.'s mother had during his birth, to his own experience at a Vermont boarding school, to his disappointment when Jr. gave up the trumpet because it hurt his lips. Joe and the teachers listened, unfazed by Sr.'s randomness. He wondered what Lynch and the students thought.

With a few minutes to go before the scheduled end of the meeting, Joe said, "It looks to me like we have a couple things at work here. One is a group of teachers who are working hard for Jr.'s benefit. The second is a student who is doing well and a father who loves his son and has very high aspirations for him, which his teachers share. At this point, I think we need to continue our communication and observation of how Jr. is doing and look toward his annual review, which is scheduled for September."

Joe hoped the meeting would placate Sr. for a few months. He had spent a lot of time talking with Kristi and the regional special education coordinator about Jr. All were convinced that the Pinicon teachers were meeting their obligations. Jeralyn and the regional coordinator felt the real issue was Sr. wanting the stage and trying to undermine his son.

To Joe's surprise, it appeared that the meeting had satisfied him. He said, "Mr. Gentry, thank you. You know how much I dislike it when I come in here and you guys waste my limited time."

"I'm glad you found our time today productive, Sr. The thanks should really go to these teachers," Joe replied. "And they've got to get right back to class, because as I said, we're short-handed today."

Sr. whispered a few things to Lynch, collected his briefcase, and shuffled out, humming what sounded like an old ZZ Top song. Joe motioned to the teachers to let Sr. go and put a little distance between them before leaving.

Lynch said she had a few questions to ask about Jr.'s case. "We'd like to have all of his documents and transcripts of previous meetings."

"Sr. sometimes records the meeting, but we don't have them. And we certainly don't have time or staff to transcribe them. That's not our job."

"Well, we'd like to have whatever you have compiled. We'd also like to get copies of the course syllabi, along with the textbooks, lesson plans, teacher credentials, and so on. It will help us put the teachers' comments in context and determine if he is appropriately placed with the requisite level of services from the district," she continued. "We'll wait while you have your staff compile them. My students can assist, if needed."

Joe had had enough. "Patricia, we had no idea you were coming today. Joe thought he could see her bristle at not being addressed as doctor or professor. "You heard the teachers, saw their notes and records. You also heard Sr. I won't be sending copies of anything today. That's not how this works."

Lynch cut him off, pointing her finger. "Understand that we're here to assist the parent in protecting his child's right to an *appropriate* education and we'd like to have the instructional materials to ensure that is happening. And I have some other questions you'll need to answer."

"Jr. is getting more than an *appropriate* education. In fact, it's beyond what's required. We allowed an hour for our meeting, which is now over, and I have some other responsibilities waiting for me. If you need to see me, you're welcome to make an appointment."

"We're here *now* and prefer to get the materials today. Again, my students can assist."

"We can't do that today, Patricia, I'm sorry. Tell your students the field trip is over."

"If that's the way you want to do it, we'll be in touch," Lynch said curtly.

Joe wished he hadn't said the last part, but he'd had all he could take. If he was required to produce copies, texts, and syllabi, it would take something more than Lynch's pomposity and condescending attitude to make him cough them up. As Lynch and her students walked toward the professor's Volvo, Joe wondered if he had made a mistake. He needed to make some calls.

THEY'RE OF AGE

"I've got a real doozy for your today, boss. And it's not even the AD's sportsmanship committee you stuck me with," Frank Young said.

"I have great hope for that committee," Joe teased. "What's up?"

"This one has a lot of twists and turns, man. Long story short, last Friday night a few kids went over to watch Liscomb High play. No worries, except that they decided to stop at The Doll House on the way home."

"The *Doll House*?"

"Yeah, the BYOB strip club right off the interstate."

"Fake IDs?"

"Nope. They're all *eighteen*."

"You're shitting me. Good one, but the joke's over," Joe protested.

"I wish. Are you ready for the kicker?" he asked.

"No. I'm not. But whatever it is, this is an athletics issue. *You* have to handle it."

"Phil Randall, the assistant girls' coach at Sherwood, is the one who turned them in. And it gets better."

"Of course it does," Joe said, shoulders slumping.

"One of the dancers is a girl from Hillcrest High. *She's* eighteen too. Amateur night."

"Good God," Joe sighed.

Young said a deputy sheriff had walked through the club and noticed beer cans at their table. "When he ID'd them, he saw that they were all eighteen, but he charged them with possession anyway. Phil Randall said he didn't see them drinking the beer but confirmed that there were beer cans around. There'll be game and meet suspensions for Eric Horn, a basketball player, and Bryce Cone, a wrestler. He was a state qualifier last year. Daniel Henshaw's not involved in anything, so nothing for him."

Young flipped open the Pinicon Athletic Handbook to the page with language about the privilege of representing Pinicon High School and that engaging in any activity, legal or illegal, that could reflect negatively on the team or school district could be considered a violation of the school's good-conduct code.

"I'll talk to the coaches and the parents this morning. Just want you to know what's going on and what a bargain Pinicon gets on my services every day."

"How are the coaches going to react? And the parents?"

"Hard to say who'll be more disappointed, the coaches or the parents."

"You'll let Zylstra's office know? Keep me posted," Joe said, still shaking his head.

Later that morning, Young reported that he talked individually with the three boys, each of whom seemed embarrassed and remorseful. He told Eric Horn and Bryce Cone they would be suspended for three contests per the handbook.

JOE'S SINS LIST

Rupert Krensky had attended Pinicon through tenth grade, but was sent to live with an aunt in Kessler during his sophomore year while his dad, Micah, was undergoing cancer treatment. Rupert's time in Kessler had apparently not gone well, and he returned to Pinicon hoping to graduate. Several teachers said they felt especially bad because he had "seen so many things as a kid." The only surprise, they said, was that Rupert wasn't even more of a problem in school.

Rupert seemed destined to follow the troubled path laid out by his family. His at-risk status, along with the struggles of Robin Stiles and a few others, prompted Joe to ask the leadership team to help him brainstorm ways of dealing more effectively with troubled students. Pinicon lacked an at-risk program, but the sharing arrangement allowed Pinicon students access to the program at Kessler. Practically speaking, however, it never seemed like much of an option, as the program was full.

Rupert was at the top of what Patrazzo dryly called Joe's SINS list—*Students in Need of Saving*. There was a time when Patrazzo's acronym would have set Joe off, but he was gaining a better understanding of Patrazzo's style. As the team discussed Pinicon's most troubled students and those who posed the greatest risk to the climate of the building, the same names appeared.

"I'd like to have the faculty compile a similar list and see who we're missing. Then, I want to challenge each of us to think about how we relate to those kids. I've tried to do that this semester when Robin Stiles has used her quiet space in the office. If we could all identify a troubled kid or two and commit to informally making more frequent contact with them, it might be a first step toward progress. It's not a substitute for a legitimate at-risk program, but a start."

The team liked the idea, but cautioned that some teachers would say they lacked the necessary time or training.

"I know. That's why I'm looking at this as a coalition of the willing. I think there will be enough that we can give it a shot. I'm opening this to everybody—support staff, custodians, bus drivers. Anyone who wants to help," Joe said.

He was pleased with the way the full faculty responded. The faculty identified a few students that the leadership team had missed, but the numbers seemed manageable. Altman, who was already bringing Mace Stallworth to school, immediately said he would give it a shot with Robin Stiles. Rhonda Prior said she got along well with Travis Rolling. Merle Richards offered to give it a shot with Daniel Henshaw and Rupert Krensky. Den Herder said he would continue to work on several shaky football players. Once they offered their services, other teachers followed suit until most of the identified students were paired with a teacher.

Prior especially praised Richards for making an effort with Rupert and suggested what he needed most was a steady male figure. "I think most of his dealings with males have been negative," she suggested. "He has so much anger inside. I worry about what might happen if that comes out in the real world."

Joe thanked the group for its willingness and said Jeralyn and the at-risk coordinator from Kessler would be coming to the next faculty meeting to share some basic techniques for connecting with difficult kids. As the meeting broke up, Richards caught Joe's arm.

"Remember how you asked about opportunities to participate in things along with the kids?" he asked.

"Sure do, but I haven't done much of it," Joe said.

"Well, since I'll be working with Rupert and he seems to need some male help, why don't you think about joining our design dilemmas project? You can be on his team. They get three weeks to identify and address a design problem."

"Merle, it's a great idea and I'd love to, but I'll be showing how little I know in your area."

"Well, maybe you'll learn something," Richards smirked.

SKYPE CONFERENCE

"Just understand that, from a parent's perspective and maybe even the professor's, the world is full of defensive educators who come across to parents like they don't want to provide services to the student. As a parent, you can identify with wanting the best for Elliott and Margaret," Kristi said in response to Joe's description of the last meeting with Sr. Zimmerman.

"Telling parents who want a Mercedes special ed program for their child but the law and budget allow for a Ford is hard. But the Ford will work if we're really doing our jobs," she said. "Sounds like you're handling a tough situation pretty well. Just stay close to the regional special ed coordinator."

"I hear you, Kristi, but I'm telling you, the kid's only disability is his father," Joe said.

"He might be, but you have to let the system work. I've got something you guys can help *me* with," Kristi said.

"Shoot," said Sutt.

"Winthrop had really bad flooding last year and it displaced a lot of families. Enrollment is still down. And it looks like a couple of the bigger businesses in Winthrop aren't going to reopen after all. We've been coordinating relief fundraisers and so on. Anyway, a mom asked me if we would participate in *Change Changes Things*. Basically, kids collect loose change for ninety days, and the national organization multiplies it by three times. The proceeds go to a partner school in a developing country."

"I've heard of it. Sounds cool," said Joe.

"Me too. Saw it on *60 Minutes* or something," said Sutt.

"So do you think we should do it?" Kristi asked.

"I don't see why not. Doesn't sound like a lot of work for you, a good lesson for the kids, and some nice publicity," said Joe.

Kristi said she was leaning away from participating. "We've got kids right here in Winthrop whose lives are still a mess from the flood. I think that is where our focus should be right now, not ten thousand miles away. My grandma used to say that charity begins at home."

"It's nice outreach, but I see your point. Is mom going to raise hell if you don't?" Sutt asked.

"Well, aren't you the political one?" Joe asked.

"Hey, I'm just being practical," Sutt responded.

"She is definitely influential and used to getting her way," Kristi said.

"Either way, you better communicate it clearly. Does the supe care?" Joe asked.

"He's pretty involved in the local recovery stuff, but just like that lawn chemicals thing last fall, he says it's a building decision. Come to think of it, he says that a lot."

Kristi asked them to weigh in on a second issue. "I've got this teacher's aide, Linda, who is pretty good with our BD kiddos. No real training, but she's got a knack for the tough ones. Trouble is, she dresses terrible. Sloppy sweatpants; big, baggy t-shirts. Just awful. In her evaluation the other day, I said I'd like to see her improve her appearance. I thought I was very calm in reasoning with her. I told her I know she is not making a lot of money, but that even the greeter at Wal-Mart looks more professional and has a blue vest."

"Let me guess," Sutt said. "She used some of the words she learned from the BD kids and quit."

"Yep. She said she could make more at Gas and Go anyway, and they get a green apron. I told her it was her choice, but that improving her appearance if she stays here was a non-negotiable. She walked out. A few parents complained to me and the super. An anonymous note in my mailbox called me the "fashion bitch."

"Forget the note if someone is too chicken shit to sign it," Sutt said.

They discussed what Kristi should do. "If she is *good for kids*, you may have to eat this one and get her back in there," Joe said. "With a little talk about professionalism."

Sutt disagreed, saying that her disrespect and stomping off shouldn't be tolerated. Kristi was torn when Sutt changed the subject.

"We had the Super Bowl of food fights. It's taken like fifty hours to sort out," said Sutt. He explained how disappointed the administrative team had been at not picking up hints of what was coming. "They meticulously planned it, down to the minute and menu. *Ravioli*."

"When the clock clicked to 12:10, it was like a freaking explosion. Stuff flying everywhere. When we saw the video we figured out it was a big-time conspiracy. Most of the kids in the B lunch group were wearing old ratty clothes. Kristi, your aide would have fit right in! A couple kids got hurt, some kinda bad. Rudy usually doesn't do lunch duty, but he happened to be in there. You should've seen him waylay this baseball player who was chucking open pudding cartons. I've never seen anything like it. He's pushing expulsion for the ring leaders. And get this—a couple of them are upper crust kids from Pill Hill. Never been in trouble, good grades. It's gonna get crazy when those parents go to the board to say Rudy is too harsh. He said this is a line in the sand and he has to know whether the board supports him. No one is saying it out loud, but the issue for some of them is that the new black principal is pushing expulsion for some rich white kids. The shit's gonna hit the fan, big-time!"

"But I've got *another* one too!" Sutt explained that an Oswald graduate in his mid-thirties living out of state had contacted Rudy about making a cash donation to Oswald High School. "He was kind of a rough kid in high school, in his share of trouble, but hit it big in business and wants to give somewhere between $250,000 and $500,000 dollars because he likes how Rudy is trying to change the place. He is especially pumped up about Rudy challenging teachers to *focus on students* and understand their lives."

"No way! That's big money! What's the catch? Is he running a Ponzi scheme or something?" Kristi asked. "There's always a catch with this stuff, right?"

"Maybe," Sutt answered. "Dude's money comes from a *medical marijuana business*. He's got a giant warehouse, a staff of agronomists, you name it. *Crazy* money. Anyway, the catch is that he was a stoner in high school and there are still some teachers here who had him. I guess they wouldn't let him walk across the stage at graduation because he circulated a parody newspaper that made shit of the principal. Others think the money is tainted because it's from medical marijuana."

"What did Summers used to say? Reality is stranger than fiction, especially in schools?" Joe asked.

"No doubt! So what's gonna happen?" Kristi asked.

"I don't know. Some people in the community are wound up. Others think it is the American Dream. I do know this dump could use a quarter-million dollars worth of paint and fixing up."

"I've got one more thing," Joe said. "I've told you guys about some of the racial/ethnic tension around here, right? I've got an idea and want to know if you think I'm crazy."

Joe explained his view that Pinicon teachers were split into thirds. "I think a third is pretty sensitive to the climate and knows we have some challenges, a second third is aware of some tension, but doesn't do anything, and another third is oblivious."

"Sounds about right. I think we have some of the same problems," Sutt said. "I don't think it's fair to assume that urban teachers necessarily *get it* because they're urban. Cluelessness comes in lots of packages."

"I'm thinking about putting a few of the new kids and their parents in front of the faculty to talk about their experiences here. . . . Things that are said and done that teachers may not be aware of. Let the faculty—and support staff too—hear it right from the parents and kids. What do you think?"

Kristi spoke first. "I like the idea, but you better be careful who you invite. You don't want them to start calling teachers out. That could make it worse."

Sutt was hesitant. "As much as it pisses me off when teachers ignore that stuff, I wouldn't do it. I think you're setting up an *us versus them* situation between those parents and your teachers. A powder keg, man. Instead, I'd collect the info from the parents and kids myself and then report it to the teachers."

Their answers were what Joe expected. And both made some sense.

QUESTIONS

1. Evaluate Joe's interaction with Karl Ortiz. Has he let the situation with his son Oliver go on too long without effective intervention or a plan?

2. Critique Joe's response to the confrontation between Heidi Morris and Diane Watters.
3. React to Joe's wish to get teachers involved in examining test scores and other evidence of student performance.
4. Assess the way Joe handled the meeting with Sr. and Jr. Zimmerman and Patricia Lynch.
5. What thoughts do you have related to Joe's request for teachers and other staff to increase their efforts to connect with potential at-risk students?
6. Evaluate Kristi's decision not to participate in the Change Changes Things fundraiser.
7. How should Kristi proceed with the classroom associate and her attire?
8. How should Rudy Carlson respond to the potential donation from the Oswald High School grad?
9. Is the parent/student/staff meeting Joe is considering advisable? Or is it a recipe for disaster?

Chapter Five

March

Capacity, Silence, Tension, and Tears

HE'S SO QUIET

Claire always said that a mother's job is to worry about her family. The first several months at Pinicon had passed quickly, and to say that Joe had become immersed in his job was an understatement. She knew he was making a conscious effort, especially since winter break, to find and protect some family time. She had settled into a three-day-a-week work schedule at the furniture store, which helped her feel professionally challenged but still in tune with her family.

Claire was delighted to find a weekend with no school activities and talked to Young about covering any major Friday afternoon blowups so she and Joe could get out of town at noon. Frank was, as always, agreeable. "I'm willing to do about anything if it will help get that sourpuss to lighten up and be a little bit more fun," Young told her. "And I'll try not to call with bad news, like I did when the $3,500 came up missing from the wrestling tournament."

She arranged for her sister to stay with Elliott and Margaret and booked a bed-and-breakfast in an offbeat, artsy town a couple hours from Pinicon. "We've got a dinner, microbrewery tour, and some art shops on the agenda. And you're getting a massage from this Norwegian woman I found on the web. I can see that you need one." Joe knew better than to argue.

At dinner, they spent most of their time talking about Elliott. "He's a quiet kid, but I can usually read him," Claire said. "And I think things have been harder on him than we realize."

"I haven't sensed any big problems from the move," Joe said.

"I don't think it's so much *the move* as it is being the *principal's kid*," she clarified. "I think he feels pulled in two directions. One group holds him to a higher standard for just about everything—school, sports, whatever, like they're waiting for him to screw up. Some others pile on the praise for what a model citizen he is. And I think a lot of kids steer clear of him because he's the principal's kid. I think he's in a hard place sometimes."

Listening to Claire's impressions, Joe felt instantly insecure. He had thought a lot about Elliott's situation, but hadn't shared Claire's level of concern. Maybe he was missing things. He sighed and refilled the wine glasses.

Claire continued. "There's always more going on with kids than it appears. You've got so many things going—kid issues, teacher stuff, Don Mitchell, the daily headaches—I can see how you can lose sight of *him*."

"So what do we do?" Joe asked.

"I want him to be his own person. He can't be weighed down by whose kid he is," Claire said.

"I'm probably too absorbed in being principal and losing sight of him a little, but it strikes me that in some ways, our challenges are the same. He's got to be his own person and not burdened by his dad's job just like I have to be myself and not the former principal or some other person the teachers might want. That's a lot for a fifteen-year-old kid to sort out," Joe said

As they talked their way through dinner, Joe remembered the connection they forged years before and how he was drawn to her common sense, intuition, and perspective. Whenever he was too caught up in something or a little offtrack, she came up with just the right antidote. Part of it was their history together, but a larger part was the way she continued to grow and, subsequently, make him better. Though he had great confidence in Kristi's ability as a leader, he marveled at how she kept herself balanced without a spouse's support.

They were the last two in the restaurant.

"No more school talk," she said.

IT'S MY FAULT

Kristi's call came on Wednesday morning, and Joe knew something was wrong as soon as he heard her voice. "I'm on my way to the hospital. Our custodian had a heart attack. The kids were out at recess and they saw him collapse," she said, voice trembling.

"OK. Calm down, Kristi. Are you in the car?"

"Yeah. I'm on my way to the hospital. I feel sick, Joe. I've been on him to get the sidewalks cleared from that heavy wet snow. At recess all the kids saw him just slump over!"

Kristi had described Earl, the veteran Winthrop custodian, as "a nice old guy, but a step slow and just a plodder." Winthrop classrooms had exit doors leading directly to the playground, but the doors had not been used in winter. "I decided we needed the snow cleared for safety. Earl wasn't happy, but I told him it was to be his top priority. I think it was too much and I pushed him too hard!"

"There's nothing you can do now but support Earl and his family. It will be fine, and it's *not* your fault. It could have happened sweeping the floor."

Joe could hear Kristi's breathing through the phone. "But I told him to get at it and was all bitchy about it."

"Kristi, you *don't know how* to be bitchy. Moving that snow is part of his job. Stuff happens. It will be fine. Call me back when you know something, OK?"

TO HELL AND BACK

Young was flabbergasted when Paul and Brenda Cone challenged their son Bryce's three-game wrestling suspension for his trip to the strip club. Eric Horn's parents were disappointed, but said nothing. Daniel Henshaw's father, Wes, just rolled his eyes.

"I was sure all the parents would be supportive," he told Joe. Instead, the meeting with Paul Cone had been as intense as any Joe had seen. Cone insisted that the boys had broken no laws, and since there was no evidence that they had been drinking, the school was wrong to hold them in violation of the good-conduct code for athletes. During the meeting in Joe's office, Cone produced a cell phone video on which the bouncer said he had not seen the boys consume any alcohol.

"I'm not too interested in a cell phone recording of a strip club bouncer," Young said. "Regardless of whether they were drinking and the charges stick, *their presence* sends a bad message for the team and our school, even if they are legally of age to be there. And our policy is crystal clear."

Joe saw Cone's jaw clinch as Young prepared to read the relevant section of the good-conduct code. He wondered if Young was coming across as too combative, but it was clear that Cone was not going to like the school's position no matter how the news was delivered.

"What's clear is that this is bullshit! I'm not gonna watch my son get screwed on this. He's broken no laws, and your fucking handbook doesn't count for shit! I'll get an injunction and go to hell and back to see that he wrestles!"

Young had reached the boiling point and snapped, "Go get one. They're not playing as long as I'm AD."

Paul Cone leaped to his feet and said, "You better enjoy it, because you may not be much longer. I'll tear this place apart and bury your asses in it," reaching out toward Young, who also stood. Joe stepped between them.

"This meeting is over. We've explained the policy and we're through listening to profanity. Paul, I need you to leave," Joe said as calmly as he could.

Cone looked at Joe and then back to Young. "I never thought I'd see two supposed-educators getting off on ruining a kid's senior year. Is this your fucked-up idea of fun? These kids have never been in trouble but you're gonna throw the book at them!" Cone hissed, pushing into Joe as he stepped aggressively toward Young, who held his ground.

"Paul, I'm asking you one more time to leave, now. If you don't, I'm calling the police," Joe said, his forearms braced in the tight space between the men.

"What a couple of chicken shits," Cone scoffed, shaking his head.

Joe held Cone's eyes, holding his cell phone in one hand and gesturing to the door with the other. Cone left.

Young collapsed back into the chair. "I never saw that coming, but he might be right about one thing. I may not be AD much longer. This isn't worth it."

Joe believed the adage that no one is irreplaceable. He also knew that losing Young as AD would be disastrous. "Just an unexpectedly bad case. No good deed goes unpunished, man."

Young shook his head. "I just can't believe it."

"Injunction or not, drinking or not, they violated the code and they're not playing. And even if we didn't have it in policy, the coach decides who wrestles. We would go down and suggest it's time for a lineup change. We're not getting pushed around by someone like Paul Cone. No way," Joe said.

HEAR NO EVIL, FIX NO EVIL

Joe had never taken a phone call *from* Karl Ortiz. Each of the couple dozen times they had spoken on the phone, Joe had placed the call, always hoping to get the timing right and catch him in a talking mood. So he was shocked when Carrie said, "Karl Ortiz is on the phone for you," with a raised eyebrow.

"We wanna talk to you. Can we come up right now?" Karl rasped in to the phone.

Joe glanced at the clock. He had an observation scheduled in Martinson's classroom in twenty minutes. Though it didn't feel right, Joe said he would clear his schedule if he came right away. He sent Martinson a quick e-mail apologizing and explaining that a difficult parent had just accepted his standing invitation to talk and was on his way.

Karl, clad in tight jeans, a sleeveless Sturgis Motorcycle Rally t-shirt, and boots, walked in with his girlfriend, Destiny. Extra-firm handshake. His son, Oliver, trailed a few steps behind, looking apathetic. Joe's office was a bit small for four people, but he slid his office chair over to the round table. "You said you wanted to find something that works for Oliver. We're here. What do we do now?" Karl asked.

Joe began by thanking them for coming in, trying not to come across as too formal, remembering how Karl liked his off-the-cuff statement about how many people probably agreed with Oliver's profane assessment of him. "We ought to start by asking Oliver how we can help him."

Joe was surprised at how comfortable Oliver seemed talking. He described boring classes and feeling like everyone looked down on him. "It's like y'all are waiting for me to screw up. Like teachers know I'm going to and it's just a matter of time. So why stick around? I just leave. I don't mind school that much; it's just the people."

"When you say people look down on you, what do you mean?" Joe asked.

"Like, if you've got money here, or if you're a jock or in music, that's cool. If you're not one of those *good kids*, then it's like get out of the way."

"Where do you get that feeling?"

"The teachers' attention goes to the good kids, the ones they like. And so if you're an outcast like me, what's the point? I'd rather quit and get a job or something."

Joe gave his standard answer, but tried not to lecture. "The problem is that *if* you could find a job without graduating, that money would feel pretty good now, but in a few years, you're stuck in the same deal. Or worse if the job goes away," Joe said, hoping Karl and Destiny weren't offended.

"He's right, Ollie. That's how you end up workin' part time at the Trailways," Karl said. "Tell him what else."

Oliver paused, seeming hesitant and uncomfortable. Joe pressed. "There must be more I need to know."

Oliver paused again, looking over Joe's shoulder and out the office window. "They say all kinds of stuff. The kids. Just names. Stupid stuff. And sometimes it just gets to me."

"Like . . . ," Joe prompted.

"They call me stuff. Tamale, stretchback, gravelbelly, you name it," Oliver blurted, clenching his jaw.

The names stung Joe like a slap across the face. "Oliver, I'm sorry. Nobody should have to hear that. This is the first I've heard of it. I want names, times, and places. I can't promise you that it won't happen again, but I'll deal with anyone I know about."

"Them teachers hear all kinds of stuff and don't do anything about it," Karl complained. "I've been around here long enough to know how it is. He's lucky he ain't more like me, 'cause I'd go upside somebody's head. He wants to go to Carville and live with his mom anyway. That's probably what he'll do. A clean start."

Despite Oliver's dismal school situation, having them in his office felt like a glimmer of progress. Oliver was more engaged than normal and Karl was reasonable. Destiny said nothing, but gave off no negative vibes. Joe took a gamble.

"Oliver, I'm gonna say something with your dad and Destiny here. I want you to think about it. You can sure go to Carville and live with mom. Sometimes a new start is a good thing. But if you stay, you could help me try to change this place. I need help with that. Without you, it might take a lot longer to change." He paused, not wanting to come off too strong or lay a guilt trip on a kid who already had plenty of challenges. "I hope you'll want to stay and be a part of something."

After several moments, Karl spoke. "Maybe Carville ain't any better, Ollie. At least *he* wants you here and maybe he's not such an asshole after all," he laughed. It seemed like a good ending point. Joe shook their hands, asked Oliver to stop in his office first thing the next morning, and suggested they be in touch after Joe had a chance see about how deep Oliver was buried academically.

As they walked out, Joe's decision to invite some kids and their parents to talk about their experiences with the faculty had been made. *We're doing it. It can't hurt.*

RADIO WAVES

"I'm not sure where things are headed with Diane and me," Mark Watters said, his vintage gray desk chair creaking as he leaned back. "We've had our issues, like any married couple, I guess. This thing with Heidi just brought them to a head. Things have probably been building for a while."

"Everyone feels bad. Heidi, me, you. The whole staff. The confrontation in front of everyone was really too bad," Joe said.

"Can I tell you something related to that?" Watters asked. "Diane and I are separated. My idea. It hasn't been easy, especially when you've been here as long as we have. Everyone feels like they have to choose sides."

"I'm really sorry to hear that, Mark. Truly."

"It is what it is. But, just an observation and suggestion. A small thing, really."

"Absolutely. Anything to help."

"I think it would be good if you could watch what goes out over the radios you guys carry. Anyone with a scanner can hear all that. So when Dave called you to say Diane and Heidi were going at it, everyone with a scanner heard that. I realize everyone knew as soon as Diane started yelling in front of the study hall kids and when we got into it outside, but I know a lot of stuff goes out on those radios. In the big picture of my life right now, it is a pretty small thing, but just something I was thinking about."

"I never once thought about that, Mark. I'm sorry that happened. Thanks for pointing it out. I'll see what options we have. In the meantime, let me know if there is anything I can do."

TIPPING POINT

Jerome Hayes was waiting for a flight at the Denver airport when Joe reached him by phone.

"I really appreciate the book you sent and I've found several good things in it. If you've got a minute, I'd like to share an idea with you."

"I'd love to hear it," Hayes said.

Joe said he may have been too slow in overtly addressing culture and climate issues related to the Kessler transfer students and ethnic tension in the building. "Whether or not we're late, I've reached the tipping point and am moving forward with a plan. I'd like you to be involved."

Joe told Hayes that he planned to invite a number of students and their parents to speak with faculty and staff about their experiences at Pinicon. "I think the best way for our folks to understand things that may go unnoticed or unaddressed is to hear from students and parents directly. There are some dangers with that approach, but we're not going to make progress without some action," Joe said.

He emphasized that he wanted the honest, unfiltered truth from students and parents without turning the session into a hazing or dressing down of teachers. "If it becomes about attacking teachers, we'll make things worse, not better."

"What is it you're asking me to do?"

"Jerome, I'd like you to participate and suggest others who should be included. I want folks who will speak honestly and directly but without putting teachers on trial or attacking them. Does that make sense?"

Hayes thanked Joe for the call and acknowledged the risks of Joe's proposal. "Let me think about it and get back to you."

Chapter 5
YOU'RE THE PROBLEM

The March air held hints of spring, reminding Joe of Professor Summers's observation that morale improved when people could "get outside and blow off some steam." Making his daily rounds, he wondered if there were studies that correlated things like student discipline referrals and academic performance referrals with seasons and weather.

He remembered the topic coming up in casual conversation at the conference principals meeting. One veteran principal had said, "We're off the wall every time there's a full moon. That's real. If you don't believe me, ask a cop, ER doctor, or nursing home staff." Joe laughed, thinking about how he had actually checked Pinicon's extracurricular schedule against the month's moon phases during basketball season. *Man, this job is turning me into an astrologer, among other things.*

His stroll through the parking lot revealed that Rupert Krensky's lime green Impala was again parked in the teachers lot. As he walked past, he put his hand on the hood. Warm, indicating he had again arrived late and not checked in at the office. Carrie confirmed that he was present in school and had not signed out for anything. Joe asked her to call him to the office.

"Rupe, how's the work restoring the Impala coming?"

"Pretty good. I'm gonna get me some rims," he mumbled.

"I kinda like the color. It's hard to miss. I see it's in the teachers' lot again today. It's gonna be towed next time. And if you're late, you have to sign into the office. You know the rules."

"I got a rule, too. Nobody messes with my car. I seen you out there with your hand on the hood. It better not happen again," Rupert said, leaning slightly forward in his chair.

Joe paused. Rupert's intense energy was close to the surface now. "Whoa, Rupe. Hang on. You know the rules. You park in the student lot, sign in at the office, and you can't have your own padlock on your locker. We've talked about all this. What's the problem?"

Rupert exploded. "You're the fucking problem!" he screamed, jumping up and shoving most of the things on Joe's desk to the floor and shattering a glass candy bowl against the wall. Joe stood in the same instant.

"Five days. You're gone," Joe said, pointing to the door. Rupert turned and slammed his fist into the door and bulletin board on his way out of the office, Joe following closely. In the hall, he pounded lockers and ripped down posters as he stormed toward the main exit, cursing.

At the doors, Rupert turned around and glared at Joe, still standing outside the office. He hesitated and then charged back down the hall toward Joe, fists clenched. "You and me, man. We're gonna go right now," Rupert growled, picking up speed.

March: Capacity, Silence, Tension, and Tears

As he closed the sixty feet between them, Joe's mind raced. *Should I fend off his punch, wrestle him out of the way, or talk him down?* The scene was taking place outside Mills's and Prior's classrooms. *Not the two best candidates for intervening, if it comes to that*, he thought.

Rupert closed to within a couple of feet when Joe extended his left arm, palm out. Doubting his gesture would matter, Joe said softly, "Rupe, this is not going to happen. Go," pointing to the exit doors.

Rupert hesitated, breathing heavily and visibly shaking. After a couple of beats, he turned and walked out, slowly this time and without pounding any lockers. As he exited the main door, Young appeared in from the south hallway. "Carrie said you might need a hand, chief."

"Thanks," Joe said, rattled. "I didn't know where that was going. Rupe just *went off*. As for you, you're kind of like a blister. You show up when the work's done," he said, trying to add some humor, mostly for his own sake.

Young laughed and hustled back to his class. Joe thanked Carrie for her quick work in summoning Young's help.

"My heart just breaks," she said, eyes filling with tears. "I've been here a while and nothing much fazes me, except kids like that. It hurts to think how kids like Rupe might end up. And we're trying so hard to help them. You're trying. We all are. But what can we do?" she asked, dabbing at tears.

Caught off guard by the extremes of emotions in a handful of minutes, Joe gave Carrie a hug. "I know. Thanks for caring," he said. "I wish I had a good answer."

"I'm sorry. You don't need me melting down on top of everything else," she said, fanning her face.

Joe sent a quick e-mail to the staff informing them that Rupert had been suspended from campus for five days and that his teachers should bring assignments and materials to the office. He popped open a Diet Coke and started writing up the incident when he heard the speaker on Carrie's phone squawk. "Carrie, Rupert Krensky is down here in the senior hall. Is he supposed to be in the building?" Den Herder asked.

"No, he's not," Joe hollered, jumping up from his desk. "Call Frank," he said to Carrie on his way out the door.

Joe's mind raced as he ran toward the senior hall. *Why does a kid like Rupert Krensky come back to school after he's been suspended and almost fought the principal? To shoot up the place* was his only answer.

Joe saw Young looking out the senior hall exit when he rounded the corner. He had gotten there first. "It's all good, chief," he said.

"What the hell?"

"Richards had his arm around Rupe and was walking him out when I got here." Young said. "Guess he needed a couple books. How about that?"

"He needed a *couple books*?"

"Not what I expected either," Young said, slapping Joe on the back. "How's your day?" he asked with a wink.

"I've had better. I don't want to say what I thought we might be in for," Joe sighed.

"That sunny optimism is what I like about you, Joey."

Joe shook his head, mind racing about what had just happened. And how to thank Richards.

IT'S ABOUT CAPACITY

"So, you're frustrated that some of the teachers aren't doing things more effectively, is that it?" Zylstra asked. "You've talked about dodgeball, outdated home ec., and boring history classes. Are those the big drags you see?"

"Patrazzo has actually come around. We're doing some team teaching. Richards and some others are using the heck out of TeachShare and working hard. And like I told you, he connects well with some of the tough kids like Rupert Krensky. Hampton is as talented as she is intense. Joyce Barry thinks it's 1950 home ec., and Petersen's a wildcard. But, Den Herder is solid and so is Altman—well, except for the X-rated banana. Morris, Watters, McCallister, Jesup . . . I couldn't ask for much more. I feel like they don't get much of my time, but probably should."

"So, listen to what you just said. You've got a couple who really struggle and a bunch who are in the middle to excellent. That's encouraging," Zylstra said. She asked if the time management software Joe had shown her could track his interactions by teacher. Joe wasn't sure.

"Have you read *Six Types of Teachers* (2005) by Fiore and Whitaker? They put teachers in three groups—Irreplaceables, Solids, and Replacement Levels. That would be a good read for you. I think most people do the best they know how under the circumstances. Your frustrations probably have to do with people's capacity and your capacity to help at this point."

"I had a conversation with Don about that but I honestly felt like he was more interested in the traditional, hammer-type principal."

Zylstra brushed off the mention of Mitchell and suggested Joe ask teachers individually to identify their greatest strengths and weaknesses. "After that, I'd ask them if they would make a joint commitment with you to be resourceful and share the things they do well—even if they're pretty basic—and then dig for some things they can improve. They might go for it if you challenge and support them. I think everyone needs the right blend of pressure and support. It's coaching. And you've got several who are already doing that with TeachShare. If you step back a bit, you may see that there's more good stuff happening than you think."

Joe speculated on how many were ready for that kind of a discussion. He wasn't sure. "I think a few of them may have so many issues with me personally, related to discipline, trust, or whatever. I don't know how receptive they'll be."

"You've been around a few months. Look at what's happening now. You see things differently than you did last fall. You've made progress. As a coach, you'd never just expect players to start making plays that are above their skill level. They've got to be *shown how*. Your job is building capacity and skill, over time."

"As long as we're talking capacity, I'll be honest. I'm not sure I have the *capacity* to help them. I know that some of what I see isn't great, but I'm not sure where to start," Joe confided.

"You don't have to have all the answers. You ask the right questions, shine the light on the issues, allow them to discover. Pressure and support. Offering to partner, providing opportunities. Find the answers together. Take baby steps forward and coach 'em up! You're well within your rights to engage them and work to identify improvement areas. Offer to be their partner in exploring ideas and possibilities together. If they're unreceptive and uninterested in professional improvement, that's a whole other conversation. That's unprofessional and a violation of standards, so the conversation changes at that point."

"Hard ball," Joe said. *Petersen.*

"Hard ball, tough love, whatever you want to call it. Continuous improvement."

Toward the end of the conversation, he asked Zylstra's opinion on putting some parents and students in front of the faculty to discuss their experiences with school climate.

"Not sure it's something I would do because it could go south in a hurry, but it's your building and you're the best one to decide what's needed. If you do it, pick the people carefully."

"The leadership team is split on the idea. I've assured them that everyone will know the ground rules and that we're not going to allow angry parents to trash anyone. This is about empathy and walking in someone else's shoes. Mostly new and minority kids, in this case."

Joe left the meeting energized, reminded that a lot of improvement often felt like one step forward. He also left thankful for the open relationship he had with Zylstra. Frustrating as his job was at times, he always left conversations with her with a little more spring in his step and a little more positive view of what was possible. *How can I interact more with her and less with Mitchell?*

Chapter 5
HONEST TEARS

"I've tried to be collaborative and share leadership at every opportunity," Joe told the leadership team, "and I know I haven't done it perfectly. I see this as a case where I'm making the call. If this meeting with parents, teachers, and kids blows up, it's on me."

As requested, Jerome Hayes supplied Joe with a list of students and parents he thought should be asked to speak. He and Joe identified many of the same parents and when approached, most were receptive. The same was not true for all of the students. To Joe, that underscored the importance of their role. *How are teachers going to understand what the kids are experiencing if they don't hear it from the kids themselves?*

In the end, he convinced several students to participate, including Oliver Ortiz. They were not to reveal names of any individuals who had harassed them or call out specific teachers that they felt were unresponsive or unhelpful; that information was between Joe and the students and families. They were simply to describe and share their experiences at Pinicon, both positive and negative.

Oliver Ortiz, though often lazy and disrespectful with teachers who pushed him, got the faculty's attention immediately when he repeated some of the slurs used toward him. That opened the door to others who shared similar, though generally less vile examples of the way they had been treated. Richard Smith's father had been the wild card, and Joe wondered if inviting him to participate would be a mistake. Joe worried he might disregard the ground rules and call out individual students and teachers, but Jerome Hayes assured him that Smith would not derail the meeting.

It turned out that Smith's words were among the most powerful. He sat silently and almost motionless in a Kangol hat until midway through the meeting. His eyes glistened with tears as he quietly described his path through school, decision to drop out, subsequent hardships, and the similarities he saw in his son's experience. "I'm afraid for him 'cause it all sounds the same," he said.

Javaris Hayes said he had not experienced much negative treatment or hostility, but noted that being an athlete helps build bridges. Jerome helped lessen some of the sting from what other families shared by saying that he actually felt better about Javaris's experience at Pinicon than the previous few years at Kessler or their time in Atlanta. "I don't believe the invitation and honest exchange we're having today would happen at Kessler. Many would rather whitewash these issues. I applaud you all for reaching out," he said.

Joe was unsure of the teachers' overall reactions, but felt that it couldn't have gone much better. "I don't know what the long-term difference will be, but the teachers who get it were affirmed, those who were pretending this doesn't happen were served notice, and those who were ignorant aren't any more," he told Jeralyn. "I had an idea."

"And what was that?"

"I'd like you to facilitate a debriefing session for teachers to talk about what they heard. Some of it was pretty intense and I think they need the opportunity to talk about it before we get together as a full group, in addition to filling out the feedback sheets. Would you be comfortable offering that?"

"I think it's a great idea, Joe."

He had also asked Mills and Prior to tabulate the results of paper and online reaction surveys teachers completed after the meeting. Mills would give them to the leadership team, which would meet with Joe within a week to process teachers' reactions and determine next steps. Joe would meet separately with support staff to solicit their reactions, and a full faculty meeting would follow.

"We might have opened up a big can of worms, but it's probably gonna be worth it," Jeralyn said.

Joe was cautiously optimistic.

SKYPE CONFERENCE

"Have I told you guys I'm learning to speak Somali?" Sutt asked. He explained that Oswald High School had recently had an influx of Somali immigrants, who had arrived with the help of two local churches and an employment agency. "We've had a helluva time getting translators. The hospital, police, and everyone in town are scrambling and the department of ed says they know of a handful in the whole state. Lucky for us there's a couple who speak decent English. I know we're not supposed to rely on the kids to translate, but we don't have any other options right now."

"So the kid is teaching you Somali?" Joe asked.

"Well, just barely. He's taught me enough to say, 'Welcome to Oswald High School. We're glad you're here,' and stuff like that. I read a welcome message and sent it out over the automated phone system the other day. Didn't reach everyone—some of our families don't have phones—but a couple of moms came in and said they had never felt more welcome in the U.S."

"That is cool, Sutt!" Kristi said. Joe agreed.

"It was, but I've gotta learn some more words now."

"What's up besides your Somali lessons?" Joe asked.

Sutt said he had spent an inordinate amount of time working with inner city students who had recently arrived from Chicago and Detroit. "I'm not sure what's bringing them to Oswald, other than the hope that they can find work and a better place to live. We've had a few more fights than usual.

When our Oswald kids check them out, the new kids don't understand that they're not rolling up to challenge them. We're trying to help the new kids understand that and teach the Oswald kids how to meet somebody new. Rudy's a big help, but it's been crazy. I've never been so ready for spring break!"

"I heard that," Joe agreed. "Look at everything we've talked about. We're not rookies anymore. I thought I was about to come to blows with a kid the other day," he said, referring to Rupert Krensky. "I suspended him for five days. I'm glad spring break will extend that a little."

"What I want to know is if you could have taken the kid or not," Sutt snickered.

"I'd rather not go there. Kristi, why don't you change the subject?"

"We talk about the crises and crazy stuff a lot, but sometimes we overlook the good stuff. I have to say things are going pretty well. I know teachers are teaching and kids are learning," she said.

Sutt agreed that each had experienced more positives than their conversations sometimes suggested. "A lot has happened since that day a year ago at the Northgate when you met with Summers, Joe. And despite the wacko stuff, most of it is pretty positive, don't you think?"

"Oh yeah. For example, I went ahead with the parents and students talking to our staff. I was nervous, but it was pretty powerful. I was worried that one of the dads might really go off, but he turned out to have the most impact. It was a risk, but I'm glad we did it. Pretty good feedback so far."

"That's a great example of what I'm talking about," Kristi said. "And what good timing to send your teachers into spring break with the parents' and kids' words ringing in their heads."

Practically, personally, and professionally they agreed that spring break had come at just the right time.

QUESTIONS

1. Evaluate the way Joe and Young handled the meeting with Paul Cone. Would it be ethical for them to declare Bryce eligible but tell the coach they do not want him to compete?
2. Evaluate Joe's conversation with Karl and Oliver Ortiz. Was it appropriate for him to appeal to Oliver to stay at Pinicon to help him address climate issues?
3. How should Joe respond to Watters's request about radio use?
4. Evaluate Joe's handling of the situation with Rupert Krensky. What should happen next?
5. Has Joe worked effectively to build teachers' capacity, as Zylstra advocates?

6. Would you have held the parent/student/teacher meeting as Joe did? What should happen next?

Chapter Six

Early April

Creativity

HOME WRECKER

Joe lingered in Patrazzo's classroom for quite a while, chatting about what had just happened. He and Patrazzo had just finished a team-taught lesson on the Great Depression, after which Patrazzo had said, "By God, Joe, I have to say that was kind of fun." They had developed a writing assignment in which students assumed various roles and wrote about their feelings after the stock market crash.

No one was more surprised than Joe to see that their relationship was improving. They were never going to be *friends*, but since their détente conversation in October, Patrazzo's facilitation of faculty meetings focused on defining the Pinicon Way and planning their way through some team-taught lessons, things had turned. Joe couldn't put his finger on any one thing as the cause. Rather, it seemed that through acknowledging his own mistakes and offering a mix of praise, ideas, and suggestions, he had opened a dialogue with Patrazzo. He was blown away that Patrazzo had become so interested in Loewen's (2007) *Lies My Teacher Told Me,* which focused on inaccurate and dull information in history textbooks. To Joe's surprise, Patrazzo was even talking occasionally with other social studies teachers through TeachShare.

Dave Crawford's gravelly voice over the radio broke Joe's reflection.

"Joe, if you're in the building, can you come to the faculty parking lot, please?"

Joe thought *what now*, but said, "Be right there, Dave."

Chapter 6

He could see Crawford and Heidi Morris standing behind the always-shiny Pinicon School's pickup Crawford used for everything. Joe often teased him that the truck always seemed so clean, he wondered how any work was getting done. It reminded him of how his granddad, Elton Rash, kept his farm equipment glistening in the same way. Like Rash, Crawford worked like a trooper and didn't know how to do anything halfway.

Joe stopped short as he walked around the back of the truck. "What the hell?" he said as Morris's red Volkswagen Beetle came into view. It had been thoroughly covered in some kind of gel, cat litter, and something else. He walked around the car, looking closely at the bubbly mixture.

"That's furniture stripper. Boiled the paint right off," Crawford said. "Stuff's slow when it's cold out, but it's warm enough today that it really took it off."

"Did you see anything? Or anyone? Find it hard to believe nobody saw anything. It's the middle of the afternoon, for God's sake."

"Neither of us saw anything, but did you see the back window?" Morris asked Joe.

"Home-Wrecking Whore" was scrawled across the car's back window. Joe sighed and looked at Heidi, who nodded slightly. *Diane Watters*.

"The power washer in the bus barn will blow that stuff right off," Crawford offered.

"We better get the police to have a look first. Let me see if the camera shows anything. Heidi, I'm really sorry," Joe said.

The video showed Diane Watters pulling into the teachers' parking lot. Though partially obscured by the Pinicon School's pickup and trees, it showed that within two minutes, Diane had slopped paint stripper, syrup, and cat litter on Heidi's car and written on the back window with soap. Lt. Beckworth downloaded a copy of the video, photographed the car, and took statements from Joe, Crawford, and Morris.

"Why would she do this in broad daylight?" Joe asked Beckworth.

"As a cop, I stopped asking *why* a long time ago, Joe, but it's a better question for you folks," he said, looking at Morris. "Is there a reason she would do this?"

Joe and Crawford left Morris to talk with Beckworth.

When the lieutenant left, Joe called Zylstra, who was not available. He left a quick message for Don Mitchell, outlining what had happened and suggesting they discuss what needed to be done to keep Diane Watters off Pinicon School property. Seeing that Mark Watters had already left, Joe dialed his mobile phone.

WE'LL COME TO YOU

"I'm going to meet Rupert Krensky and his dad at his shop in Kessler. His dad's not able to drive and catches a ride up there at 5:30 in the morning," Joe said. "Rupe's been going up there during the suspension. Is the old man as tough as I've heard?"

Jeralyn smiled. "Well, let me go with you. I've got a decent relationship with him. Rupe has probably cooled down, but who knows with those two. I can help smooth things out. We don't want too much testosterone in the air, anyway," she teased. "Plus, if it goes well, I'll take you for ice cream. I know how much you like a good butterscotch malt."

"You know how to deal," Joe said.

"I have to say, Joe, that I like your willingness to meet people on their turf. I thought it was great when you went down to the Trailways to meet with Karl Ortiz. This is probably important if Rupe's going to have a chance to graduate."

"I don't mind doing it, but I understand how some people see it as giving special treatment to certain kids or families. I went to Kessler last fall with the idea of welcoming the transfer kids, and some people were pissed off. I don't think I told you that Mitchell called to ask why I was at the Trailways in the middle of the day. He made it pretty clear that he didn't think it was appropriate. But if it helps build connections with some of those tougher cases, I'm good with it. I just wish I could get him to call me about something he likes or that we're doing well."

Jeralyn smiled. "It's an example of how you have to define the job the way you think it should be done. Sure, Mitchell is your direct supervisor, but you have an awful lot of freedom. I think you do a pretty good job of using it. Let's face it, sometimes, it's better to ask forgiveness than permission, especially from a guy like him."

I NEED A LITTLE MORE TIME

Joyce Barry held a giant stack of catalogs and flyers on her lap. She had asked Joe if he had a minute and took a seat across the desk before he could answer. Joe caught himself continuing to type on his computer as she sat.

"What's up, Joyce?"

"I think you're aware of all the issues we're having with one of our suppliers.

Their computer system has went haywire and all of our orders are wrong."

The grammatical error made Joe cringe.

"The orders for my program are wrong. Because of all of the trouble, I don't have my purchase orders ready to turn in. We're also gonna need a new oven. I know those were due before spring break but could I have another week? I don't want to make a mistake and order the wrong things, but that computer won't let me in. It's all online now. You can't even call!"

"Will a week be enough? And maybe someone could look at it with you."

"A week should suffice," she said, collecting her catalogs to leave.

"Ok. Thanks for being thorough and making sure we don't order the wrong things and lose instructional time," Joe said, a bit irritated that she had not thanked him for the extension.

"By the way, Joyce. What's your policy on late homework?"

She paused at the door. "I don't accept it—without a good excuse," she added quickly.

"I thought so."

She paused, looking a bit confused. "And your point is?" she asked, a bit defensively.

"Might be a good time for reflection, Joyce, that's all. Get me the POs as soon as you can and let me know if I can help," Joe said, picking up the phone to call no one in particular.

THE TOP 100

Joe enjoyed it when teachers came to talk about new lesson ideas. He had promised that he would always make time for these conversations and asked teachers to hold him to it. He wanted these conversations to be held in classrooms whenever possible, as opposed to his office. There were a handful of Pinicon teachers he thought would never take him up on it—at least not for a while, but a few came around quite often. Allison Jesup was one.

Squeezing into a one-piece desk with a ceramic top, Joe thanked her for the invitation. Though he hadn't liked English in high school, Joe enjoyed being in her classroom. "By the way, thanks for putting that Top 100 Books to Read Before you Die list in the mailboxes the other day. That was cool," he said. "Based on the list, I've got some work to do. I was thinking maybe we should make it a contest. Whoever has read the most on the list wins something."

"Funny you bring that up," Jesup said. "That's sort of what I want to talk to you about. A few of us were thinking it would be fun to build on that in all subject areas. You know, like find lists of the top 100 places to visit before you die, the top 100 inventions of all time, top 100 composers, artists, whatever. We thought maybe we could use it as a way to get some faculty excitement and look for connections between subjects."

Joe needed more conversations like this. "Allison, I love it. *Love it.* Maybe rather than *finding* the lists on the web, we could come up with them ourselves or develop them by departments. Or get the kids involved. You guys have such great ideas! Why don't you pitch it to the leadership team and see what they think?"

Joe was amazed at a number of things. First, that the teachers, when given the opportunity, were such a good source of new ideas, most of which didn't cost any money. He was surprised that Pinicon had never done anything with teacher leadership. *How can any principal miss out on something like that?* Second, how easy it had been to build a leadership team. He had thrown a lot at the team and the entire faculty, but most seemed to embrace the opportunity. His main challenge was not to put too many things in front of them and remember Summers's observation that the principalship is a marathon, not a sprint.

THE BOY'S REAL SORRY

Joe and Jeralyn arrived at Krensky Auto a little after 10 a.m. Micah Krensky and the shop fit the picture in Joe's head with vintage cars, mostly Chevys, in various stages of restoration. Micah's muscular, tanned arms were covered in tattoos, his thick black hair falling to his shoulders. Jeralyn broke the ice as she got out of the car, hollering to ask if he had any bargains. He gave Joe a firm handshake after wiping some of the grease off his hands.

"You must be a Chevy man," Joe said, gesturing to several old Chevrolet signs hanging in the shop.

"Oh yeah. Always was."

"And Rupe is too, fixing up that Impala," Joe said.

"Appreciate you coming up since I don't drive right now," Micah said. "The boy has something to say."

Micah wanted to get right to it. Joe had been prepared to talk through the specifics of Rupert's suspension, his academic progress, and so on.

"I'm real sorry for what I done. I won't cause no more trouble," Rupert said, shifting his weight awkwardly.

"And," Micah said sharply.

Joe suspected that most of what Micah said to Rupert came sharply. Rupert looked up from the ground, met Joe's eyes, and offered an awkward teenage handshake.

"I appreciate that, Rupe, 'cause it's not easy to do. Apology accepted. We came up here because everybody who is suspended and their parents have to meet with me to get back in school. We all want you to graduate and you're close. You'd be the first in your family, right?"

Rupert nodded.

"We don't want anything to get in the way of that, not grades or behavior or . . ." Joe was searching for the right words, not wanting to sound too formal. Micah and Rupert Krensky were not formal people.

"What he means is no more bullshit, Rupe," Micah said. "And there won't be any," he added, looking at Joe. "I told him that Pinicon was the best place for him, but he wanted to stay at Kessler. When they said he was going back to Pinicon, I was glad. He needs to graduate."

Joe stopped. "What do you mean *they said he was going back to Pinicon?*"

"That director or whatever he is. The big guy. Said things had went better when Rupert was at Pinicon and Kessler wasn't working out. He was right. He needed to be back at Pinicon where he belongs."

Joe's wheels were turning quickly. Was Rupert Krensky like Mace Stallworth in that both had been troublemakers at Kessler and were thus *sent* to Pinicon by Mitchell? It seemed so, but right now, he needed to focus on clear communication with Micah, who seemed sincere.

"Rupe, I was looking at your file the other day and saw that if you pass everything, you're within a couple of credits from being able to graduate. *A couple.* That's a history class and PE."

"Yeah, him and that *Pizetti* never got on too well, that Italian history teacher," Micah said.

"Well, he wouldn't have to take the class with Mr. Patrazzo. Kessler offers some summer courses that he could take. On the computer, on his own," Jeralyn said.

"We're short a couple guys and I gotta have him here working this summer. And we ain't got a computer," Micah said. "Maybe he could do it at night at the library or somewhere."

Joe paused. "What about this? I used to teach history. What if Rupe came back and worked with me on the history class. I'd set up some things for him to do that could count for the PE class. If he did that and we had *absolutely no trouble*, he could be done *this year*. Graduated."

Rupert looked up, curious. Jeralyn smiled cautiously.

"I mean assignments turned in, getting to school on time, car in the right lot, no padlocks on the locker, no sneaking a smoke, *not bringing anything to school that's not supposed to be there,*" Joe said. "Any slipups, and the deal's off, no graduation, and he'd have to take the computer stuff in the summer or come back next year."

"You hear that," Micah asked his son. "You got a chance. Hell yes, he'll do it."

"Dad thinks it's a go, Rupe, but what do you say?" Jeralyn asked.

Rupert nodded quickly. "I can do that."

"You got an opportunity," Micah said, looking at his son. "Don't screw it up," he said, motioning for Rupert to shake hands with Joe again.

The four chatted a bit more, with Jeralyn lightening the mood and getting a few smiles out of Rupert. Micah seemed to enjoy answering Joe's questions about his business and old Chevys. Back in the car, Jeralyn asked how much of the plan Joe had conceived in advance.

"Not much. I hope you didn't think I was trying to undercut you or playing 'good cop-bad cop,'" Joe said. "If we don't get Rupe through right now, he's not going to finish. And I guarantee he'll get more than that online stuff anyway. I don't think we'll have any trouble from him going forward."

"Maybe not, but a lot of things have been an uphill run," Jeralyn said. "The family is legendary. And he's *two credits* short of graduation. He needs one in history and one in PE. The PE thing you're setting up would only be half a credit, so if he does it, he's still short half a credit."

"I know. But the way I see it, if he buys in and does what we ask, he's close enough in my book. Best for the kid, best for Pinicon," Joe said, wondering how she would react. "What we really need is better access to a program that can really serve kids like Rupe. We're not there yet, so in the meantime . . ." Joe left his own statement unfinished.

Jeralyn said nothing for a few minutes before breaking the silence. "Did Micah say that Kessler *sent* Rupe back to Pinicon? What's up with that?"

"I've talked to a few people who said Mitchell or someone at Kessler did that. Like they were just pushed off. Rupert, Mace Stallworth, Richard Smith for sure. I can't see Murphy at Kessler High doing that but I could see Mitchell shipping his undesirables to Pinicon. Those families don't know how to play the game of school. They're going to do whatever they're told to do."

"But we haven't had any *real* trouble with the Kessler transfers," Jeralyn said.

"True. Mace Stallworth is kind of an outlaw, but most are like Javaris Hayes and just wanted a change. I think a handful are refugees that Mitchell or somebody wanted to get rid of. That we haven't had any real problems is a credit to the kids, the Pinicon Pals, and our teachers. Pinicon *is* a better place for them. I think that loser Mitchell is dumping kids he doesn't want on us and railroading folks who don't know their options."

Jeralyn frowned, unsure about Joe's conspiracy theory. "What is it with you and Mitchell?" she asked, shaking her head.

THERE'S A BOMB

Curt Muller had been in Joe's office a few times. Since he wasn't involved in any school activities, his interaction with Joe was limited to minor infractions here and there. For that reason, Joe had built a decent rapport with him. Curt said he couldn't wait to get out of school.

Chapter 6

Carrie had left early with a migraine when Curt walked into Joe's office during seventh period. Despite the chaos that sometimes accompanied the secretary's absence, Joe was enjoying the quiet afternoon and the chance to read a couple articles Kristi had shared on Twitter. The soles of Curt's shoes squeaked on the tile as he walked in. "Uh, Mr. Gentry? You got a second? I've got something here you'll probably want."

"Sure, Curt. Come on in. What's up?" Joe asked, looking up from his screen.

Curt handed him a white trifold paper towel Joe recognized from the Pinicon restrooms. "I found this in the bathroom," he said, resting his hands in his pockets. Joe unfolded it. Scrawled in black ink was written, "There is a bomb in the school."

Joe snapped to attention, not because he feared an imminent explosion, but because he had been immersed in the article on the pros and cons of student laptop computer programs and had been only half listening to Curt. He sat down and flattened the crease in the paper towel, looking directly at the scrawled message.

"Where'd you say you got this?"

"Just now. In the bathroom in the senior hall."

"Anybody in the bathroom when you went in?"

"Nope."

"You hear anybody talking about the note . . . or a bomb or anything?"

"No. Nothing."

"Huh. This is something. Tell you what, Curt," Joe said, sliding a blank piece of paper his way. "Since you are the one who found it, I need you to do something. Write *there is a bomb in the school* for me on the paper. You got a pen?" Joe asked, padding around his desk in search of one. Curt looked quizzically at Joe.

"Cause that would help rule things out. *You*. One of the first things people will say is that the guy who found it probably wrote it. And so that would help rule you out."

"Oh, yeah," Curt said. "It was right there on the counter."

Curt produced a ballpoint and wrote as directed and slid the paper back across the table. Joe was flying blind. Yet, even if someone else had brought the paper towel, Curt Muller would be a person of interest, Joe thought, not because he was a likely bomber, but because he could see Curt making the threat.

The letter t's on the paper towel and Curt's paper were identical, as both had been made with a single upstroke, loop, and cross to the left. Both were also a bit smudged with globbed ink. Joe looked at both for several beats. Then, he gambled, turned them around, and slid them to the middle of the table where Curt could see them side by side. "Interesting, huh?"

"What? The same ink?" Curt asked.

"Well that, yeah, but look at the smudges and the letter t. They're identical. And not the way most people make their letter t. I don't know if I've ever seen anyone do it that way," Joe said, rising to close his office door. "Is there something you want to tell me, Curt? And before you answer, it's just you and me here. Nobody knows you're here. Nobody knows what you've shown me. If you wrote it, we can handle it and it ends right here. No one else knows."

He paused and tried to let the words hang there, without being overdramatic. "If not, I've got to get the police here right now, because this is a big deal. We're talking *felony*, Curt. That's *prison time*."

At that point, Curt became defensive and agitated. "What the . . . you think *I did it?* I went in to take a piss and you think I did it? Why the hell would I do it?"

"I'm just checking, because the police are going to ask the same things in about two minutes. If you're sure, grab a seat in the detention room while I take a look at the cameras."

He called Zylstra's mobile phone and breathed a sigh of relief when she answered. He badly wanted to avoid involving Mitchell on this. "Carol, I know Don's my direct supervisor for day-to-day stuff, but this is beyond day-to-day. A kid just brought me a paper towel that says there's a bomb in school," he explained. "I'm 98% sure he wrote it and it's nothing, but I'm calling the cops to come up here and talk to him. But we can go with our plan and evacuate if you would rather. You're the boss."

Zylstra wanted to know how he was so sure. Joe told her about Curt and the identical letter t's, the smudged print, and Curt being left-handed. "I don't want to be on the six o'clock news, Joe."

"I know. I really thought I could break him. I'm sure the cop will."

"You say you're 98% sure, huh?" She paused. "Alright. Get the police up there but keep it quiet. I'll be there in ten minutes."

Joe was glad that he had cultivated a comfortable relationship with Lt. Beckworth, through the homecoming vandalism, missing money from the wrestling tournament, and vandalism of Morris's car a few days before. Joe appreciated that Beckworth regularly stopped by the school, just to be seen and chat. "It's not like there's a lot of organized crime on the streets of Pinicon. I've got the time," he had told Joe. The lieutenant and superintendent arrived at almost the same time.

Standing outside the detention room, Beckworth looked at Joe and Zylstra and spoke quietly. "You can evacuate, and we'll do a search right now. Tell me what you want to do."

"Why don't you talk to him and follow your gut," Zylstra suggested.

Beckworth quizzed Curt while Joe pretended to scribble some notes and Zylstra watched. After five minutes, Beckworth gestured for Joe and Zylstra to step out with him.

"I'd say this is your guy. He's nervous as a cat. I'll take him to the station and call his mom in. I'm sure he'll fold. But if you want to evacuate and search, just say the word," Beckworth said, looking at both of them. "Your call."

"Go ahead and take him. We'll sit tight. I think you two are right," Zylstra said.

Beckworth returned to the detention room and told Curt to come to the police station with him "to file a report and make a statement."

"Am I being freaking arrested?" Curt asked, eyes wide.

"No, Curt. We've gotta file a report since you found it," Beckworth said.

Once at the station, Beckworth called Curt's mom and increased the pressure. "Like Mr. Gentry said, people are gonna suspect you, so I've got to understand exactly what happened," he said. Thirty minutes later, Curt folded and admitted writing the note on a whim, but only after Beckworth left Curt and his mom alone in the interview room.

"I'm not sure I would do it this way again, Joe," Zylstra said. "We could've evacuated and had the same outcome. But I trusted that you and the cop had a good read on him."

"Do you think I mishandled it?" Joe asked.

"No. It would have been on me if we were wrong. We got it handled. Seems like the kid needs some help. We'll recommend expulsion and send him to the alternative program."

"Some of our Pinicon kids need better access to that," Joe added, seizing the moment.

"So, here's a leadership question for you," Zylstra said, popping open a Diet Coke. What would you say to the board member who asks why we *didn't follow* the policy and evacuate but *are following* the policy regarding expulsion?"

"Are you asking rhetorically or for real?"

"Does it matter?"

Joe paused. "I'd say we didn't evacuate because the language in the policy talks about the threat being *credible*, which I didn't think it was."

Dr. Zylstra smiled and held out her hand. "For the record, I agree. You were in a position to make that judgment. All of this is a judgment call. You knew the policy, followed your gut, but also checked yourself with me and the cop. Making the right calls with no time, under pressure, and without all the relevant information is what your job is all about. You did all that, and today we won."

RUMOR MILL

Jeralyn strode into Joe's office with a fresh plate of cookies. "I've always believed that a well-fed principal is a happier principal," she said in her chipper voice. "Return the plate and I'll refill it."

"That won't take long," Joe said. "You're bouncing around like you never even had surgery."

"Good as new. *The Power of Positive Thinking*, but that's way before your time. I brought the cookies because I have one of those uncomfortable counselor/principal deals to share."

Jeralyn said she had talked with a few high school girls about a rumor that Jr. Zimmerman and Savannah Shottenkirk had an encounter in the wrestling room the day before. "It could be nothing, really big, or something in between. I know those two are headaches by themselves. It's too bad they got together."

"Pfff, let's hope they didn't *get together*." Joe paused while Jeralyn caught the double meaning.

"I mean the two headaches combining to form one bigger one," she said.

"Believe me, I know what you mean," Joe said, shaking his head.

It had to be investigated, but it seemed anything involving Jr. Zimmerman rose to a higher level of concern, because of Sr.'s propensity to stir things. The same was true for any member of the Shottenkirk family. Joe asked Jeralyn to run down the specifics of the rumor. "Savannah and a few girls are interested in Jr., or claim to be, or maybe they want to make her jealous. Who knows," she explained.

"Perfect," Joe said sarcastically as he inhaled another cookie. "Have you talked to either of them?"

"No. Savannah never talks to me."

And Sr. has never liked me because I told him one time that Chinese or Spanish would be better second languages for schools than German."

"Seems reasonable to me," Joe said. "Alright, I'll see what I can find out. My instructional leadership will have to wait. *Again*."

Joe's first disappointment came when he realized that Jr. had been in Petersen's PE class during the time of the alleged rendezvous, while Savannah had been in Barry's fashion merchandising class. *Petersen wouldn't notice if the President of the United States walked into the room*, Joe mused. *I hope Joyce was paying attention.*

To Joe's surprise, Jr. had actually *signed out* of Petersen's class at 1:47 p.m., but never signed back in. Petersen said he knew Jr. was back in for the end of class at 2:02 p.m., because he "had to yell at him to turn the stereo down." Barry had no written record, but knew Savannah had gone to the restroom near the end of the period. Neither teacher noticed anything unusual about the students when they came back to class.

Chapter 6

Joe went through his usual process of talking to Jr. and Savannah, trying to make it as low key as possible. He didn't want them to know he was specifically investigating the rumor, so he said he was looking into a restroom light fixture that had been damaged and that he needed their help since Pinicon's security cameras did not cover that part of the building. He began by telling them that the amount of time they'd been out was too long. Jr. admitted he was "kind of stalling because Petersen's class is so boring." *At least he's honest about something*, Joe thought.

When Joe mentioned the rumor, Jr.'s eyes widened and he seemed embarrassed. "Nah. That's just talk. She likes me, though," he said. When Joe asked if he had seen or talked to Savannah while signed out, he said that he had. "She was down by the locker room," he said. "She, like, asked me if I wanted to hang out or whatever in the wrestling room. But I didn't." When Joe asked directly if he had talked to or spent time with Savannah, or if there was anything to the rumor, he said no.

Savannah told Joe she had "to take care of personal, female things," as if he might not understand. She said she had to go to her PE locker to "get something" out of her bag and that the PE locker room is more private. *Reasonable*, Joe said to himself. She said she only saw a couple of seventh graders as she left Mrs. Barry's room. The seventh graders confirmed seeing her.

Joe told Savannah she was gone from class too long and that she should use the restroom in the nurse's office if she is feeling ill or needs extra privacy. "When students are gone for a longer-than-usual time, it makes problems. Something comes up missing, they wind up a suspect. Rumors get started."

"The nurse *isn't here* Tuesdays and Thursdays after lunch," she snapped. *Just like* mom, Joe thought, remembering several unpleasant encounters with Susan.

Joe asked about the rumor. She rolled her eyes. "Yeah, everyone is saying a bunch of stuff and it's BS. Some of those seniors are *way* jealous." Asked if she had seen or talked to Jr. while signed out, she said she had seen him at the drinking fountain when she came out of the locker room.

She looked at him incredulously when he asked if the two of them had been alone together. "If you're asking if we did something or if we . . . no. *I'm sure*."

Joe was torn. No one near the wrestling room had seen either student, nor had Crawford and the other custodians. Joe's experience with both families was complicated. *Do I have a nasty high school rumor, something consensual in the wrestling room, or a sexual assault?* Savannah was shifty, but usually easy to read. Jr. was less credible, and Joe's relationship with him was no better than with his father. Joe thought it likely that Savannah had invited Jr. to waste time near the end of class—a theory Jeralyn also favored.

"I don't see Savannah doing anything. Sex, I mean, but she'd love the rumor, because it's a little racy and might get Jr. thinking about her. And Jr.'s a goof, but he's pretty harmless," Jeralyn said.

Joe called McHale for some guidance. "Talk me through this, Tom." After explaining what he knew, Joe shared his conclusion. "I think it's a stupid rumor. I don't think anything happened and there's no way to know if something did. So I think I'm moving on. I don't want Sr. to find out, blow a gasket, and bring Patricia Lynch and her students in here again. Does that sound reasonable?"

"I think so. You investigated, and decided it was a bunch of high school talk. Principals do that kind of thing all the time. Are you going to do anything with Jr. and Savannah, discipline-wise?"

"Other than warn them about losing sign-out privileges from class, no. I think anything I do would just get people wound up unnecessarily. I think it's pointless."

"Are you treating these two differently from the way you would handle other students?" McHale asked.

"Well, yeah. You've seen Sr. and Susan in action and know what I'm talking about. Am I doing this wrong?"

"I'm just asking the question. Something to think about, that's all," McHale said, sensing Joe's frustration. "For what it's worth, Joe, I think you're fine, so long as your *hope* for this to be nothing didn't lead you to *determine* it was nothing. Some would say you have to give them some kind of sanction because other students would get one. I just hope there's not more to the story somehow."

Joe thanked McHale and took a chance on catching Sutt and Kristi at their computers. After hearing the background, Sutt's advice was direct. "That, Joseph, is the definition of a sleeping dog. Let it lie, document your investigation, and forget it. Asked about how to handle Sr. and Susan if and when they learned of the rumor and his investigation, Sutt said, "Tell her you checked, decided it was unfounded, and that you don't bother parents about every stupid high school rumor that comes up."

"I'm glad that your mentor asked if you were treating this kid differently than others, and I'm glad he asked if your *wanting* it to be nothing influenced your conclusion," Kristi said.

As he clicked off the screen, he thought about the number of times in grad school when he and his classmates had wrangled with concepts like equality, fairness, ethics, and the influence of context on a given situation. *Those were all easier to solve back then*, he thought.

Chapter 6
EFFECTIVE IMMEDIATELY

It was unusual for the meticulously organized Zylstra to call an administrative meeting with little notice. When a 4:00 p.m. meeting of all Pinicon and Kessler administrators and directors was called, speculation ran wild. "I'll bet she's got a new job. It's that time of year," Tom McHale said as he and Joe pulled into the parking lot outside the Kessler Central Office.

A silence fell over the room as Zylstra walked into the board room in the Kessler Central Office. Joe noticed newly added aerial photographs of the Pinicon school buildings hanging next to similar photos of Kessler facilities. Zylstra was, as always, dressed in an expensive looking suit. *She certainly looks the part if she's got a big new job*, he thought.

"Thanks for being here on short notice. You know I try to be respectful of your time because principals never have enough. I've said several times that the principalship is the most difficult job in school administration, but you're not going to get me to walk into the debate about whether elementary or secondary is more difficult." She smiled as the principals laughed.

"That depends on the superintendent," joked one of the Kessler elementary principals.

She then got to the point of the quick meeting. Please forgive the formality of this," she said as she unfolded a small sheet of paper from her suit pocket. "It'll work best if I just read it. Without going into too many details, I have been diagnosed with breast cancer. Some of you know that I have a family history with the disease, which makes my doctors insistent that I begin aggressive treatment immediately. I am scheduled for surgery later this week, followed by chemotherapy and radiation. This will take me through the end of the school year because of a few complicating factors that I won't get into. All of my treatment will be done at the University Cancer Center and I have great confidence in the team there."

The room was silent as she continued, her voice catching. "I also have great confidence in the team *here*. The bulk of my duties will be shifted to Don Mitchell, whose experience has been invaluable to me. I have met with the central office staff and board to ensure that disruptions for principals and teachers will be minimized. I know you'll continue to work together for the good of our Pinicon and Kessler students. With luck, I expect to be back to work as soon as possible, though the doctors refuse to give me a time frame. I appreciate the wonderful work you do for our students and also your prayers as my family and I prepare for the road ahead."

Silence again permeated the room as Dr. Zylstra collected herself, cleared her throat, and, rather awkwardly, invited everyone to enjoy some refreshments and conversation. As she did, the administrators stood to give her a standing ovation, causing tears to well in many eyes, including Zylstra's. Joe chatted with a few other administrators before he and McHale drove back to

Pinicon for Joe's presentation with the Pinicon Optimist Club on school volunteer opportunities. Neither felt much like talking. Joe's mind raced about how his work might change with Zylstra's absence.

McHale broke the silence and reflected on the superintendents he had known. "Other than a few things that were grossly mishandled, she's been the best supe I've worked for," he said. "She's pretty tough. I bet she'll come through this fine. And, I don't think Don Mitchell can screw too many things up as a short-term fill-in. I'm sure she gave him some clear instructions," he said.

"I'm a little ashamed to admit one of my first thoughts was what it would be like to have Mitchell in charge," Joe confided. "That's pretty selfish, given what she's up against."

"Nah. Principals balance so many things at once. Stuff comes out of the blue all the time. It's easy to fall into a pattern and become a little self-absorbed and miss the bigger picture. I'm not worried about you missing the big picture because you're reflective and honest."

They agreed it would be interesting to see what Don Mitchell would do as acting superintendent.

READING AND LEARNING

Joe had been pleasantly surprised that Mark and Diane Watters's marital problems seemed not to have impacted Mark's teaching. The couple had separated but were in counseling together, and Diane had not returned to school. Joe had sent her a certified letter, informing her that she was not to return to school without an official invitation from him. He hoped that would be enough to keep her away.

"You know how much I like getting asked to talk about a teaching idea, but let me first tell you what a great job you've done focusing on your students through all of this with Diane," Joe said. "I'm sure it hasn't been easy."

"Actually, it has helped me refocus," replied Mark. "I'm trying to pour myself back into improving and trying new things, if that makes any sense."

"Whatever the case, you've handled things like a real professional," Joe said.

"Thanks, but I'm here to get your take on an idea. You're always wanting us to push the instructional envelope a little, right?"

"Absolutely," Joe said, reminding himself of the buckeye and his ongoing efforts to be more direct and less filtered.

"Ok, tell me what you think. A few of us are talking about a sixties unit that includes civil rights, the anti-war movement, technology, music, books, you name it. We're using stuff from the Empowering Educators Conference and TeachShare. Believe it or not, Patrazzo's even interested!"

"I like it. Keep talking," Joe said, leaning forward in his chair.

"OK. I found an article I'm thinking of using with the seniors. Alex Haley, who wrote *Roots* and co-authored *The Autobiography of Malcolm X*, did an interview in 1966 with George Lincoln Rockwell, the founder of the American Nazi Party."

"Wow. You guys are hitting on all cylinders! Primary sources, a giant of American literature, a controversial subject, and a flaming racist. You weren't kidding about pushing the envelope!"

"So you're OK with it?"

"Absolutely. I don't think we're helping kids learn if we aren't honest with them. And we *are* talking about seniors. Maybe it can help us deal with some of the racial/ethnic stuff. I'd like to get involved like I did with Helen's class when they read *The Things They Carried*. I loved it! Let me know if there's a way for me to be involved."

"Great! Now that you're onboard, one more thing."

"Shoot."

"Is it OK that the article is from *Playboy* magazine?"

Joe raised an eyebrow, perplexed. "What?"

"I know, but Joe, the thing is fabulously written . . . by *Alex Haley*. But I'll scrap it if you want."

"Let me think on that one. I liked it more when I thought it was from *Newsweek* or *Time*."

THE BIRDS AND THE BEES

"I call this the Birds and Bees talk, because it comes every spring and the principals are always afraid I'm going to tell them about pregnant students," Jeralyn said.

"Principals are always on guard. What can I say?" Joe asked.

"*Well . . . ,*" Jeralyn replied.

The levity left Joe quickly as Jr. Zimmerman and Savannah Shottenkirk and the wrestling room rumor jumped back to the forefront of his mind.

"We do have one such situation to discuss, yes. Michelle Gabus," Jeralyn said, while Joe exhaled. "Why are you looking at me like that?"

Joe sighed. "I thought you were gonna say Savannah is pregnant."

"Good Lord, no," she said. "Michelle is a sweet girl, really bright, but I worry about her. Boyfriend graduated a couple years ago. I didn't expect this, but we're dealing with kids here. You never know. I hope it doesn't make her family situation even tougher. She's got a lot on her plate."

"I assume you do some direct work with kids in her situation?"

"Oh yeah, and I have a good relationship with her, but I had another thought. What would you think if I mentioned your wife? Do you think Claire would be comfortable talking with her? Michelle might benefit from knowing there is a successful woman out there who experienced some of the same things. Michelle's gonna have a lot thrown at her when this all hits."

Joe paused, trying to remember if he had told Jeralyn about Claire becoming pregnant with Elliott at nineteen. He was fairly certain he hadn't.

"I did the math, Joe. I'm sorry if I made you uncomfortable. I knew Claire had to be young. Just a thought," she said.

"No, that's fine. I couldn't remember if we had talked about that. Claire's not a counselor, but I'm sure she'd talk to her if you think it would be good. Will her parents be OK with that?"

"Well, it's just an idea. Poor Michelle's never had a role model, and mom and dad are pretty hands off. Talk to your wife and I'll talk to her folks. The only other thing we need to talk about is prom. I'm sure the ballots for prom king and queen will be different from homecoming."

He had wondered whether Jeralyn remained uncomfortable with the way he had manipulated the homecoming votes in October. "You do know that Rich Eshler will be bringing his boyfriend from Hillcrest to the prom, right?" Jeralyn asked. "They have been dating a while and were going to come last year, but changed their minds at the last minute. They were afraid we wouldn't let them."

"Nobody could have stopped them. *Legally*, I mean," Joe said.

"Well, *they* didn't know that and were afraid to, even though I told them to go for it," she said. "I don't think it's a big deal. Everyone knows Rich is gay. In fact, he and Travis Rolling will probably be bringing you the paperwork to start a Gay-Straight Alliance. I'm proud of those two. We've needed that for a while now."

"I hear a lot of principals say GSAs really help with their climate. Murphy says that's the case at Kessler," Joe said. "Do you think anyone will object?"

"Hard to say. I got out of the prognostication business a long time ago. All I know is that I'm proud of those kids," she said.

SKYPE CONFERENCE

Kristi seemed almost more concerned about Dr. Zylstra's coming absence than Joe. "Oh, no." Kristi gasped. "She's so good. Who's taking over for her? Will it affect you much?"

"Don Mitchell, the associate superintendent, will take over. We'll see. He's kind of a hacker, but he usually forgets about me and Pinicon unless he's getting phone calls."

Joe shared the story of Curt Muller and the bomb threat, wondering how Mitchell would have reacted had he been in charge.

"That is the single best school story I've ever heard! Gentry, you're *the man*! How did you come up with that? You must watch a lot of TV," Sutt said.

"It just came to me, but I don't know if I'd do it again. I'd still make him write it and lean on him, but we might just evacuate. I'm not sure the supe was totally comfortable. I'm not sure I would have been, in her shoes."

Sutt and Kristi were amazed at the turn of events between Mark and Diane Watters and Heidi Morris. "It is so true that we spend so much time being social workers."

"It's a sad deal. We had to send Diane Watters a certified letter explaining that if she came on school grounds without an invitation, we'd call the police. The insurance company totaled Heidi's car. Watters's wife put stuff in the gas tank and everything."

Sutt asked if Mark Watters's teaching had been impacted.

"I don't think so. He's really good. If anything, he's gotten better because he is really pouring himself into his job. In fact, he was in here asking me if he could use a 1966 *Playboy* article for a class with the seniors," he said, explaining the story.

"Say what? Are you gonna let him use it?" Sutt asked.

"I haven't decided. I feel like I need to support their efforts to try new, creative things. Even Pat Patrazzo is coming around. But I do wish the article were from someplace else."

"*Patrazzo*? Isn't that the guy who was gonna fill out the grievance after you got into it with him? That's awesome. What's been the difference?" Kristi asked.

"Maybe some time. I offered to partner on some stuff with him, like the team teaching, and I think that helped too. But the biggest thing might be his role on the leadership team. I couldn't believe they voted him on there and I was worried he might be toxic, but he's embraced it. I don't think teachers have had those opportunities here before."

"Sutt, what do you have from this month's episode of As Oswald Turns?"

"We've got this girl in the junior class—I'm glad she's not one of my freshmen. She's pregnant, and the baby is due this summer. She's really smart, super quiet, a little goth. No one knows who the dad is. So get this," Sutt continued. "We just found out the whole thing *is fake*."

"What do you mean, fake?" Kristi asked.

"I mean she's not pregnant! She's been faking the whole thing since fall. She bought some pregnancy suit online and has been changing her size and shape all along."

"How was she getting around PE? Wouldn't somebody see her changing clothes?" Kristi asked.

"Nope. Had a letter from a nonexistent doctor saying she should not participate."

"She need some counseling? What's going on with her?" Joe asked.

"She saw one of those experiments on TV where they go around and see how they're treated. She wanted to try it pregnant."

"She'll probably be a famous sociologist or something," Joe predicted. Then Sutt dropped the bomb.

"Funny you say that, Joe, because she's in a dual credit sociology class at the community college and their adjunct teacher *knew about it*."

Kristi and Joe gasped at the same moment. "Get out!" Kristi shrieked.

"Apparently, it was the girl's idea, but the teacher knew what was going on and they were talking back and forth about it the whole time. Pages and pages of stuff between them."

"What's happening with the teacher?" Joe asked.

"Not sure. She only teaches there part time. Rudy wants to put all of our dual credit courses with another college, but one of our board members is a VP there. Freaking politics."

"That shouldn't matter, but what a mess," Kristi said.

"I agree, but let me ask the out-of-bounds question," said Joe. "How was she treated? I mean, a lot of the famous sociology studies from years ago revealed all kinds of stuff, but you could never do them now."

"That's what I've been telling Rudy. This is a teachable moment for us. I told Rudy to look at what it shows about Oswald High School. I told him it fits with him wanting us to understand what it's like to be an OHS kid. But Rudy's hard headed and pissed off, so I'm tiptoeing."

The three debated the merits of Sutt's idea for several minutes before Kristi changed the subject. "Earl, our custodian who had the heart attack, isn't coming back. Said he just can't keep up, and he and his wife want to do some traveling anyway. I still feel bad, though, but let me tell you about how we're doing faculty meetings."

Kristi said she had begun recording videos of herself presenting information prior to faculty meetings. "Sometimes I'm pointing out certain things in an article I want them to read. Then, at the end of the video, I pose a few questions for them to reflect and write on. When we meet as a faculty, the focus is small and large group discussion and their reactions."

"That's awesome," Joe said.

"They looked at me like I was crazy when I told them about it. I actually look *forward* to faculty meetings and I think they do too. I'll send you a link to a blog that talks about it."

"I wasn't going to say anything, but since we don't have any secrets between us," Joe said, "let me tell you about a deal I made with a student. He then told Sutt and Kristi about the deal he had made with Rupert Krensky. And the debate began.

QUESTIONS

1. Evaluate Joe's handling of the incident involving Morris's car. How should he proceed?
2. Is Joe right to give Barry more time in determining what supplies to order? React to his question about whether she allows late homework.
3. Evaluate Joe's visit with Micah and Rupert Krensky and the plan he offers.
4. Critique Joe's handling of the bomb note.
5. Assess Joe's actions involving the rumor surrounding Jr. Zimmerman and Savannah Shottenkirk.
6. Should Joe allow Watters to use the article from *Playboy*?
7. How might Zylstra's departure impact Joe? Should he do anything differently with Mitchell serving as interim superintendent?
8. Is Jeralyn's suggestion that Claire talk with Michelle Gabus appropriate?

Chapter Seven

Late April

Never Saw That Coming

CREDIT DUE

Joe and Richards had reduced their early morning meetings to about once a week, as Richards had been spending more time on TeachShare and felt that Joe's time might be better spent elsewhere. As the spring semester had rolled on, both felt good about the direction of Richards's classes and his students' behavior in class.

"I've gotta tell you that I never thought I'd look forward to seeing you in my class. Thank you for the time you've spent down here. It has really helped," Richards said, sipping his coffee.

"I've just been sharing and listening, Merle. You're the teacher, and that's where it all happens. Truth is, it shouldn't have taken me half the year to get out of the police role and into a supportive one. I was new. . . . Well, I'm still new, but I'm learning. The whole thing's a process. I appreciate that you were open to the conversations. Wish everyone was."

Richards said he had to get a few things ready for the morning and needed to cut the chat short. As Joe stood, he spoke.

"One more thing and I'll get out of here. I know you and Mrs. Martinson put in a good word with Rupert Krensky. I appreciate it. It probably made all the difference for that kid. He's got a chance to graduate and do something. Thanks for that and for getting him calmed down and out of the building the day he went off. There's no substitute for those connections."

Richards smiled slightly and shrugged. "How'd you know that I..."

Joe cut him off. "Have a good day, Merle. And thanks again."

Chapter 7
OUT OF THE BLUE

"I think maybe she is coming around, Carrie," Joe said, referring to Jodee Tursi, who had just left his office. "Would you believe she wanted to know if she could bring her cat to Allison's class? They've been reading Hemingway and that got them started talking about Hemingway's cats. So she asked Miss Jesup and she sent her here. Have you ever known Jodee to be interested in *anything* school related, much less English?" Joe asked, playfully.

"I can't say that I have, but I've always liked Jodee and her brother. I went to school with their mom," she said.

"I guess Miss Jesup wins the prize for getting her interested in *something*," Joe said.

At about that time, Carrie's phone rang. "Hi Marty. He's right here. Hang on. Marty Beckworth for you," she said, transferring the call to Joe's office.

"Marty, I hate the feeling of dread I get every time I hear your name," Joe teased. He wondered if Beckworth would be interested in becoming a full-time school resource officer if Joe could find the money. *I'd love to get the Kessler grant writer working on that.*

Beckworth laughed. "We have similar jobs sometimes. People aren't automatically glad to hear from us. I do wish I was calling for another reason," he said, suddenly more serious. "I've got a buddy in the department at Kessler who told me they picked up Gregg Altman last night."

"What the hell for?"

Beckworth said Altman had been arrested for shoplifting trail mix. "Apparently the managers at Super Foods have been watching him for months. He fills up the bags and writes a dollar amount that is way less. Does it with all the self-serve stuff they have up there. Coffee, candy, whatever."

Trail mix? Joe thanked Beckworth but wished that he had heard the shocking news from Altman, even though the source wouldn't make any difference. He called Altman's cell phone and left a voicemail asking him to stop in his office as soon as he arrived at Pinicon. As he hung up, Murphy called. "You talked to Altman yet?" Murphy asked.

"No. I just got off the phone and left a message for him. What is going on?"

"He was just in my office. He resigned. The guy had tears in his eyes when he left."

Thirty minutes later, Altman was in Joe's office. He turned in his keys to the building, the driver's ed car, and a pile of Pinicon Pirates coaching gear. "Someone might as well have this stuff. I'm sure you wouldn't want me wearing it around." Altman had a blank look.

"I don't get it, Gregg. Are you having money problems?"

"Not any different than any other teacher," Altman said flatly. "I won't try to explain it away, Joe, because there isn't a decent explanation. I started grabbing a thing or two here and there. Stupid stuff, like granola bars or ChapStick. Kinda told myself I worked so hard teaching and coaching that it wasn't a big deal and I deserved a break and the stores wouldn't miss it. But I'm pretty competitive and it became like a contest." He paused, looking at the floor, eyes glistening. "I know how stupid that sounds."

"Fair enough, Gregg. I appreciate the good work you've done here," said Joe, stunned that the trust he had in Altman had evaporated. *What else is undiscovered with this guy?*

"I know you tried to support me on the banana deal. I appreciate it. Maybe among my other faults, I just have a judgment problem. It was stupid and this is just . . . anyway, I'm sorry." With that, Altman extended his hand, shook Joe's, said goodbye to Carrie, and walked out of Pinicon for the last time.

Over the next three weeks, Beckworth told Joe that Altman was "as close to a serial shoplifter as anyone's ever seen. The guy is blacklisted all over this part of the state. Nothing he takes is worth much by itself, but it looks like he hardly pays for anything."

PUMA CONCOLOR

Joe had just finished sending an e-mail to Mark Watters telling him to proceed with using the Alex Haley interview from *Playboy*, with conditions.

> *First, send a message to parents telling them we talked about it, that Haley is an icon of American lit and that the article will be read from a clean copy or whatever—aka not photocopies from the magazine. Make sure they know the kids won't be checking out the centerfold, etc. Be clear that the content of the article could be offensive on many levels but that it addresses some big goals of the course, that these are college-bound kids, etc. Tie it to the curriculum. And to contact one of us with any concerns. Let me take a look at the letter before you send it. —JG*

Sixth period had just begun as Joe passed by Jesup's tenth grade English classroom. He heard Jodee Tursi talking to the class, but what he saw made him do a double take. Jodee's older brother, Alan, who was a couple years out of school, stood at the front of the classroom. In his arms, he held what looked like a young mountain lion. It was clearly not full-grown, but couldn't be called a cub.

The cat was squirming actively when Joe walked in. It howled so loudly that Jodee and Alan didn't hear Joe the first time he said, "Get that thing out of the building."

They heard Joe's raised voice the second time, though he tried not to startle the cat, which was no longer content being held by Alan, who wasted no time in heading for the door, as startled students slid their desks to make way. He hurried down the hall with Jodee scrambling nervously behind, dragging their jackets, a duffel bag, and some kind of harness.

The cat let lose full-throated howls, prompting curious teachers and students to peer out of their classroom doors. Joe called Carrie on the radio as he followed them down the hall. "All teachers close their classroom doors, *right now*. Close all the *interior doors*," he said into the radio, suddenly remembering Mark Watters's complaint that everyone with a similar radio or police scanner could hear him. *I've got to do something about these damn radios.*

"If that thing gets loose, you two are going to jail," Joe hissed as Alan tried to wrestle the cat into submission and Jodee hurried ahead to open the exit doors. *I wonder if Beckworth can capture a mountain lion loose in the building.*

"You said it was fine," Jodee protested. "I told you I was bringing him."

"Don't start with me, Jodee. You don't want to go there."

Once outside, Joe saw Crawford talking with the Pepsi delivery man, who was complaining that Alan's car was blocking the loading dock. Crawford started to ask Joe if he knew whose car was in the way. "Gentry, what's goin' on?" he yelled, not believing his eyes. The Pepsi man looked similarly confused, unable to process what he was seeing.

Jodee had produced a large pet carrier. "Forget that. He's not gonna go in there, just open the car," Alan yelled at his sister, panic in his voice, barely able to handle the struggling cat, which was now in full protest. "Open the goddamn door!" Jodee fumbled with the keys, opened the car door, and leaned the seat forward enough for Alan to stuff the howling cat in and slam the door shut.

"Jodee, my office. Now. Alan, you're not coming back to school without a personal invitation from me. You got it?" The cat paced the backseat of the car, pressing its nose against the rear window, fogging it up. Jodee disappeared back into the school while Alan stood around, waiting for the howling cat to calm down before trying to get into the car.

As Joe turned to walk back into the building, he saw Dave Crawford and the Pepsi man both doubled over with laughter. Joe couldn't help laughing, though he tried to conceal it. He jumped back on the radio and told Carrie to let the teachers know their doors could be reopened.

TOTALLY SHUT DOWN

Joe's phone vibrated as he sat in Rhonda Prior's geometry class. Students were working in small groups on projects demonstrating how geometry could be applied to fields as diverse as manufacturing, fashion, sports, and advertising. *How awesome would it be to have a school full of Rhonda Priors?* he asked himself. Glancing down at the phone, he saw Kristi's text message: *Call me ASAP. Sutt in hospital.*

He resisted the temptation to slip out immediately and make the call, but there were only fifteen minutes left in the class. He had told Carrie that only bombs, blood, or bullets should get in the way of his time in classrooms, and she had done a great job of protecting his schedule. As the lesson wrapped up, he gave Prior a quick nod and confirmed that they would talk about the observation after school. He dialed Kristi on the way into the hall.

"What's going on?" he asked.

"Sutt's wife took him to the hospital. He woke up this morning and couldn't move."

"What do you mean, couldn't move? Like stiff getting out of bed?"

"She said he was completely immobilized. She and the neighbor got him to the car, and they're doing a bunch of tests now. She said she'd call when they knew something."

Sutt had always thrived on little sleep and lots of action. Both Joe and Kristi admired the way things seemed to roll off his back, and the thought of him flat out in the hospital didn't fit. Joe's mind raced as to what might be wrong and he wondered how to best support Sutt and his family. Distracted, he kept checking his phone and tried to make the rest of the day and postobservation conference with Rhonda Prior productive.

Kristi called again that night. She had spoken with Sutt's wife. "It's really weird," Kristi said. "They're calling it *reactive arthritis*. Some kind of virus that settled in his joints. They're gonna keep him a while and do a bunch of tests because they're not sure that's what it is."

"I've never heard that," Joe said. "What do you think about a quick trip to see him?"

"Actually, I was going to ask you the same thing."

They agreed that spending a personal day visiting Sutt was a good idea and arranged to meet at an interstate rest stop and ride to Oswald together the next day. Joe called Mitchell and made a late night trip to his office to ready a few things for Young, who would be in charge. He was out the door at 6:00 a.m. the next morning to meet Kristi.

The time in Kristi's Prius flew by as they compared notes on difficult teachers, curriculum improvements, Elliott, school politics, the potential benefits and problems with 1:1 laptop programs, and their average number of work hours in a given week.

"We haven't even touched on the personal stuff, like life balance," Joe said, describing the calendar Claire had been keeping that showed Joe's work and family time. "Color coded and everything."

"And how did it look?"

"Not great, but better than last fall. We try to have a date night at least once a month and we're doing OK if you count trips to Target. It's been better since I put those on my work calendar and block them off just like meetings and school stuff, but sometimes I'm just too tired, and a trip to Target is no substitute for meaningful time."

They were silent for a few miles as billboards rolled by. "Kristi, don't take this the wrong way. You know I love my family, but there have been times when I've envied you and *the time* you have to get things done without feeling guilty for not being at home. I know that's crazy and sounds awful. I feel guilty even saying it. How messed up is *that*?"

"It does sound horrible, but I know what you mean. Funny you bring it up, though, because I can't count the number of nights and weekends I've sat in my office, wishing there were someone waiting for me to come home. Since there isn't, I just work more. And we both know you could go seventeen hours a day and never be done."

Joe agreed. "They tell you in grad school and you know it's true, but only after you're swimming in it do you realize how hard it is to find that balance."

"As long as we're being so honest, I'll put a couple more cards on the table," Kristi said. "Because people don't see me with a boyfriend or husband, apparently some have decided I must be a lesbian. A board member came to see me last week and did everything but ask me directly."

Joe sat, speechless, alternating his wide eyes from Kristi to the interstate, which was funneling down to one lane because of construction. "What the hell?"

Kristi said the board member was "nice about it," but that he was clearly concerned about perceptions in the community and on the board. "He said over and over that he thinks I'm doing a great job and they're glad I'm here. Just kept talking about *people's ideas*. Never used the *l-word*. I think he's afraid to say it."

"So what did you tell him?" Joe asked, still incredulous.

"I was disgusted but I hid it pretty well. I thanked him for the positive feedback on my performance and for coming to see me. I also told him the way I spend the small amount of time left when I get home from Winthrop Elementary is *my business*. I probably should have told him I just haven't met the right man, but I thought, *no way. Let them wonder*. I told the supe it was pretty weird. And I wrote the whole thing down in my journal."

"That's bizarre. I've never once thought about that, but I'm sure there are tons of issues for unattached administrators."

"And *female* ones," Kristi added. "Or gay ones."

"Does it make you worry about your job? Or want to leave?"

"Not a bit. I'm a little offended, not that somebody suspects me as a lesbian, but that they think it's *their business* and some wacko has the guts to ask. And it's a school board member!"

At the hospital, Sutt's appearance surprised them. He was pale and had put on fifteen or so pounds since they had seen him in December, but the changes hadn't shown up via Skype. He was in bed, back at an angle, with SportsCenter on TV. He was more than a little glad to see them.

"I'd get up for a hug and a manshake, but you might never get me back into bed," he said, visibly stiff and uncomfortable. Joe and Kristi wanted to avoid interrogating him, but it was hard not to. Sutt's answers to their questions revealed a struggle he had kept hidden.

"I've been so busy, just like you guys—long hours missing meals and workouts, eating terrible. At night, I'd pull in the garage and close the door behind me to avoid talking to the neighbors 'cause I just didn't have the energy. I'd try to spend some time with Jen and the kids before they went to bed. Then I'd work for a couple hours, which got me wide awake, so I'd have a few beers and get lost in my iPod, thinking that was *my time*. Next thing I know, it's 3 in the morning. Off to work at 5:30. That was my pattern for a few weeks and all of the sudden I couldn't get out of bed. It scared me, man."

They stayed with Sutt for a couple hours and, though they tried to talk about other things, the conversation kept returning to school. Sutt pleaded with them to stop the Kristi-lesbian story because he was laughing so hard it hurt. "I'm sorry, Kristi. You know I'm not laughing *at you*, but you *cannot* make this shit up. Unbelievable," he said before entering into a coughing fit.

Joe and Kristi told Sutt goodbye and made a quick stop to see his family before getting back on the road. It was a long day, but they were used to long days, and the time flew. The conversation on the way home centered on the future, life balance, and the lives of principals. Back at the interstate rest stop, they lingered a few minutes before heading home.

"This was really good. I'm sorry Sutt had to land in the hospital for us to get together again," Kristi said.

"I know. Let's finish strong and regroup this summer," Joe said.

"Yep. Thanks for today, Joe. It was really great. I love you guys."

"Back atcha."

BLINDSIDED

"Line two is for you," Carrie said as Joe's phone lit up.

"Good morning; this is Joe Gentry."

"What the hell was going on with that tornado drill yesterday?" a male voice growled.

Caught off guard, Joe scrambled. "Ah, who am I speaking to?"

"Doug Benson. I wanna know what kind of asinine plans you've got sending kids in to that locker room for the tornado drill. Absolutely ridiculous!"

Joe asked Benson to calm down and explain what he was upset about. He eventually said that his seventh-grade son's PE class had just gotten out of the showers when the locker room filled with junior and senior boys because of the tornado drill. Joe explained that the locker room was a designated tornado safety area that had always been used as such.

While talking to Benson, Joe pulled up their family information on his computer and could see that he was a surgeon in Kessler. "It's completely inappropriate to have those senior boys come storming in there while prepubescent boys are standing there naked, trying to get dressed! How 'bout a little common sense? You're lucky the tweet those thugs sent didn't include pictures. I don't know why you allow kids to have phones at school anyway. And if *my kid* got stuffed in a locker, there'd be hell to pay."

Joe asked for some specifics about the tweet, who was stuffed into a locker, and if his son had been bothered in the locker room. Benson knew no specifics about the tweet or who had been shoved in lockers. Joe said he appreciated the call and that he would investigate.

His first stop was with Stu Petersen, who said there was some "horsing around" in the locker room but nothing unusual. Talking with students revealed that two seventh-grade boys had apparently been shoved into lockers before Petersen got to the locker room. When Joe followed up with Petersen, he said he had dealt with it at the time.

"What did you do?" Joe asked.

"I got the seventh graders out of the locker and told the seniors to knock it off."

Joe told Petersen it wasn't enough. He found the tweet using his Pirate-Guy account and questioned a few more kids before suspending two senior boys and confiscating their phones, much to the chagrin of their parents, who felt Joe was overreacting. Petersen maintained that the problem was Joe's fault because of an ill-conceived tornado plan.

"When the tornado alarm sounds, everyone is supposed to drop what they're doing and get to their designated area and account for their kids. If you had been in the locker room on time, as assigned, this wouldn't have happened."

"It's pretty obvious that you've been trying to undercut me ever since that deal with Travis Rolling last fall. I'm a marked man and can't do anything right in your book," Petersen complained. "I'll just send everything to you now if you're going to second guess my discipline."

"Stu, I don't have a choice but to document this in your file. You were late getting to the locker room and, as a result, two kids got shoved into lockers, and your only response was to get the kids out and yell at the seniors. That can't happen. If there's a legitimate reason that you can't perform your supervisory responsibilities, I need to know that."

"Well, duh, that's what happens when you mix seventh graders and seniors in there for a tornado drill; bad things are gonna happen. The problem is your tornado plan, not me."

"Stu, I know the locker room will be crowded in a tornado situation, and I'm not crazy about mixing the ages. I know that's uncomfortable for those middle school kids, but the building has been inspected by the county emergency services people, and they say that is the safest place. Until we have a safe room or better spot, that's the way it is. The teacher has to be there to account for the kids and to *supervise*. Plain and simple. I've got to have you there on time, every time, period."

Petersen turned and left Joe standing in the PE equipment room.

FOLLOW PROTOCOL

"What exactly went on with your emergency lockdown the other day?" Mitchell asked over the phone. The call caught Joe flatfooted. He didn't know what Mitchell was referring to.

"When you had everyone close their doors."

"Ah, that. It wasn't an *emergency lockdown*. It was a classic snow job," Joe said, half laughing as he described the incident with the adolescent mountain lion. "I walked by the English room and saw it and told them to get it out of the building. I suspended the kid who misled me about what she meant by *cat* and told her older brother that he's not coming back to school without a personal invitation. If he shows, the Pinicon PD will help him leave."

"So you had a *mountain lion* in the building?" Mitchell asked.

"That we did. Not a lot of first year principals can claim that," Joe said dryly.

Mitchell's prolonged silence told Joe he saw no humor in the event itself or in Joe's retelling. "For starters, you must not have looked at our animals-in-school-facilities policy."

"No, I can't say that I did."

"We've got a policy, Joe, that relates to an identifiable educational purpose and curricular connection, advance notification of parents, veterinarian certification, that it's on a leash or in a carrier, and so on. When McHale's reading teachers have kids read to dogs, all those dogs are approved. This is basic management stuff."

"I'm sorry, Don. I never once thought of any of that. I assumed the kid was talking about Fluffy the cat. I really did."

"Doesn't matter if it is Fluffy. You know how to spell *assume*? And you know what it means?" Mitchell asked.

"Uh, I do, yeah."

"A-s-s-u-m-e. It makes an *ass* out of *you and me*," Mitchell said. "I've got to document this in your file, Joe. You telling everyone to lock down went out over the radio, and we looked really stupid and that's not OK. You get paid to administer policy and you need to know what it is and follow it. That thing gets loose and we've got a . . ."

"I *get it*, Don. Point taken," Joe said firmly, burned that Mitchell was treating the mountain lion screw up strictly according to the book, while blowing off so many other things. "It didn't get loose and we stayed out of the news," Joe said.

"We probably won't be so lucky twice. Think things through, will you? We'll talk later," Mitchell said and hung up.

Joe was on fire and called McHale to vent.

"The guy has never once talked with me about anything remotely related to teaching or learning. But he's on me like a hawk over piddly little stuff like the homecoming vandalism last fall and the missing money from the wrestling tournament. Hell, if the cops can't figure that one out, how am I supposed to? And now he's going by the book with the stupid mountain lion!"

McHale told Joe he had every right to be angry. "I'm glad you called. I can feel your anger through the phone, but in his defense, not all of that is piddly. Listen Joe, Mitchell's an old-school manager and that's about it. And he likes power. He is what he is, but let me ask you something. What do you think are the most important aspects of your building?"

Joe paused. "The climate . . . one that supports teaching and learning . . . teachers collaborating and improving. Kids who want to be here. Maslow's Hierarchy of Needs. That kind of stuff."

"Good answer. In your heart, think those things are happening? Be honest."

"I *think* so. I *want* to think so."

"They absolutely are. Take a look. You've got a leadership team—something Pinicon's never had before—that has some momentum and is putting out some good ideas. You're pushing teachers to figure out what they mean by the Pinicon Way. You've worked hard to make the new kids feel like they belong, and you're providing teachers with new opportunities to grow, using TeachShare, looking at scores and some data, and all that. I think that's a pretty good start. A throwback manager like Mitchell is probably not going to see or appreciate that stuff, so don't beat yourself up over what he says. You've had some bumps and setbacks, but that's part of the deal."

SECRET DEAL

After Doug Benson had ripped him for having senior boys descend on the boys' locker room while seventh graders were dressing, Joe asked a consultant at the school division of the state office of emergency preparedness to examine Pinicon Secondary's tornado safety plan. He had just finished a phone call with the consultant when Pat Patrazzo and Stu Petersen tapped on his office door.

"Got a minute?" Patrazzo asked.

"Sure, fellas. Come on in," Joe said. Joe's relations with Patrazzo had improved markedly over the last few months, but the same could not be said for his interactions with Petersen. *What are these two gonna want?*

"We don't wanna take a lot of time, so we'll get right to it," Patrazzo said. "What exactly are the arrangements you've made with Rupert Krensky in terms of graduation?" he asked, while Petersen stood, arms crossed.

"He's working one-on-one with me on a history and PE class. He needs both to graduate. Rupert's a little bit of a special case. I put the plan in place when Jeralyn and I met with Rupert and his dad in Kessler. If he goes the standard summer school or online route, I don't think he'll ever graduate. Why?"

"Seems pretty unusual. A degenerate kid who's short on credit getting independent study course with the principal," Petersen said. "Why would he not have to follow the same path as everyone else who's short of credits? Pat and I teach the classes he flunked. Seems like he should have to take them with us, like everybody else."

The special treatment thing again, but they have a point. No one else has this kind of deal. But no one else is Rupert Krensky, and he needs to graduate and get out of the building.

"I know. The bottom line, fellas, is that he needs to graduate and be out of this building as much as we need him to go. His dad said it didn't go well in your class, Pat. And I can imagine he doesn't give a lot of effort in PE," Joe said. *I can also imagine what might happen if you get in his face about it, Stu,* Joe thought. "It's an adjustment that I think is in his best interest as well as ours. And the whole thing's on me, no one else."

"I don't know about Stu, but it doesn't bother me that he's not in my class again. I just hope we're not letting an outlaw slide by because we want him gone. It's a potential academic integrity issue," Patrazzo said.

Joe was torn between showing them the specifics of what Rupert was doing for the history and PE credits on one hand, and just nodding and listening on the other. *I don't need to justify the arrangement to them,* he told himself. He opted for something in between. "I've got him doing a big family history project and some weights and wellness stuff with me. The family history, as you know, is a challenge."

"I think this is something the faculty needs to talk about," Petersen suggested.

"I'm fine with that," Joe lied, not wanting to open the issue to the whole faculty. "As you know, we don't have a formal at-risk program, which is why I asked everyone to consider a couple of shaky kids they could try to connect with until we have better options."

Joe felt like he could justify his actions to the leadership team first, including Patrazzo, and doubted Petersen would ever bring it up. *Time will tell,* Joe thought. *Petersen just wanted to catch me in it. Plus, the faculty will love having Rupert out of the building. Patrazzo just had to go along with him.*

SMOOTH PROM SAILING (?)

Taking a break on the hiking path around Pinicon Lake, Claire scolded Joe for assuming something problematic would arise related to the upcoming prom. Joe said he often felt like the principal's job is to prepare for the worst and hope for the best. "That way, you're prepared no matter what happens."

"Fine," she said, "but stop *dwelling* on worst-case scenarios. If something happens, you'll deal with it. No more work talk. Done," she said, taking a seat on the bench alongside the trail.

Claire's words proved accurate. The leadership team had agreed that citizenship and other factors should be considered in eligibility for homecoming and prom recognition, but recommended asking the student council to form a committee to study the issue and recommendation for the following year. The student council enthusiastically agreed, though Joe's ultimate goal was to eliminate the prom king and queen entirely and instead incorporate some kind of spring service learning project around prom time.

"You'll probably get what you want, but will have to wait for it," McHale predicted. "But that's a good thing because then it's *their thing*, not something you forced on people."

Counting the votes for prom king and queen proved to be quick and easy and the ballots revealed clear winners—students with whom Joe and Jeralyn were both comfortable. Jeralyn also said that she anticipated no negative reactions to Rich Eshler bringing his partner from Hillcrest High School to the dance. "And the best thing is that the post-prom party belongs to the parents," she teased. "You'll be home by midnight."

On the Friday of prom weekend, Carrie arranged for flower and balloon deliveries to be kept in an empty classroom rather than the main office. "We were completely overrun at homecoming and Valentine's Day. The kids can pick them up after school. I've got a Pinicon Pal from study hall opening the room for deliveries when they come." Joe thanked her for the efficiency.

He was shutting down his computer a little early since he and Claire had planned a cookout with Carrie and her husband. Carrie jumped at the chance to leave a few minutes early but threatened to come back and retrieve him if Joe didn't follow closely behind. He was getting up to leave when Rich Eshler stuck his head in the door.

"Mr. Gentry, do you have a second?"

"Sure, Rich. Just on my way out, but what's up?"

"I just want to say thank you for letting me bring my boyfriend to the prom tomorrow. We thought about it for a long time and weren't sure it would be allowed at Hillcrest. And Travis Rolling and I are going to bring the paperwork to start a GSA. Mrs. Kramer said you would be OK with it."

Joe thanked him and said preventing their attendance at prom or squelching the GSA was never a thought. "I'm glad you'll be there," he said, "and a GSA will be good for Pinicon."

"I guess if everyone looked at it that way, things would be easier. And I wouldn't have to buy prom stuff somewhere else," Rich said.

"What do you mean?" Joe asked.

He said Pinicon Floral and Gifts had told his date that they would not deliver flowers to school for Rich.

Stunned, Joe said, "Jeez, Rich. I'm really sorry about that. I . . .'

"It's fine. It's not a big deal and not your fault. We bought flowers in Kessler. I'm just saying thanks. Our prom will be more fun than Hillcrest anyway."

"His principal must not know the law very well, but like I said, I'm glad you'll be there, Rich. Have fun." *Nice kid,* Joe thought. *I sure hope nothing bad happens.*

Joe and Claire enjoyed the cookout with Carrie and her husband. All three were surprised when Joe told them what Rich had said about the flower shop. "I'm not surprised that Rich said thank you. He's such a good kid," Carrie said.

"That's a good one to end on," Claire announced. "I'm declaring an end to the school talk. Carrie, you will help me enforce the moratorium, won't you?"

"It's about time," Carrie's husband agreed.

They avoided most school talk for the rest of the evening.

The next day's weather was "Chamber of Commerce Perfect," Young said. To Joe's relief, the prom was nearly perfect as well. For several years, Pinicon had hired a police officer to be present as a deterrent to student misbehavior. The students knew the routine well, and everyone arrived on time and without incident or suspicion. None of the chaperones reported any problems.

Joe grew more comfortable as the night wore on. The DJ abided by the order to play only radio-edited versions of songs. Several principals in the conference had complained about "grinding" and "dirty dancing" at their proms, but Joe encountered no such problems, at least not according to his standards. And he saw no signs of hostility toward Rich Eshler and his partner from Hillcrest High, Bryan. In fact, a good number of them cheered enthusiastically when Bryan put on what Mark Watters called "a first-class dance clinic."

After the last students and chaperones had left the gym, Claire teased, "Are you sure you don't want to help at the post-prom party? They could probably work us in dealing Blackjack."

"I'll pass, but I thought our kids were just great. It was really fun to see them have a good time."

"Are you saying you've lost some of your dislike of homecoming and prom, Mr. Principal?" Claire laughed.

"I'm not going that far," he cautioned. "But I am proud of the kids. It was a pretty good night."

SPOTLIGHT

Jeralyn had spent some time with Michelle Gabus and her parents talking about Michelle's pregnancy. "Breaks my heart that Michelle is such a good girl with so much potential but her parents are just emotionless, like they're in a trance. But, they're OK with her talking to Claire."

"She's happy to help out, but she's not a counselor. Can you help her with what to expect?"

"Absolutely. We're just trying to let Michelle know that there are people who care and she's not the only one to ever face this."

An assignment for Barry's careers class provided a convenient opportunity for Michelle to engage with Claire. Students were to interview an employed mother to learn about her experiences. "It's actually not a bad assignment," Claire told Joe, describing the visit. "She seems like a nice girl, and it took quite a while for her to loosen up. But she has no idea of how to care for a baby."

"I'm sure that's why Jeralyn wanted her to meet you. Maybe you can open her eyes a little. I guess it can't hurt," Joe said.

Though the visit had gone well, Joe hadn't anticipated Elliott's reaction. Or more correctly, the way some others would react to the principal's wife talking with a pregnant high school student about her own experiences as a nineteen-year-old mother. Elliott brought it up the next night at dinner.

"Mom, are you helping Michelle Gabus or something? Like, with her baby?"

"Jeralyn thought maybe I could help her a little, because I . . . *we* were once in similar shoes, but it was different for us because I had a lot of support. She doesn't have much. Why?"

"Just wondered. A couple people were asking about you talking to her and all that."

Joe cringed. He knew Claire would be pumping Elliott for information and that he was unlikely to share a lot. While she and Elliott were putting away dishes, Joe and Margaret moved off into the family room to play. Sensing an opening, Claire took the opportunity. "It seems like me talking to Michelle makes you uncomfortable."

"It's just one more thing, you know? Like one more thing for me to be in the spotlight."

"How does it put you in the spotlight?"

"I just do my thing, but everybody's watching all the time. Like Sam Shottenkirk the other day. He's like, '*I hear your mom is counseling that skank Michelle Gabus. Didn't know your mom was knocked up early too. Guess you guys aren't so perfect after all.*' Everyone looks at me differently because dad's the principal."

Claire paused while Joe cringed, trying to listen over Margaret's prattle in the next room. "El, people say terrible, hurtful things. I told Michelle I know what it's like and I feel for her. But I had a lot more support than she does. How did it make you feel when Sam said that?"

"Like I wanted to punch him, or at least say something back."

"Why didn't you?"

"I dunno. I would've at least said something *last year*, but dad wasn't the principal then. It's not too good for the principal's kid to get in trouble. It's like there's a different standard for me. Not something you and dad put on me, just other people. It's the reason some of them don't invite me to stuff. They think if I know stuff, they'll get in trouble. Or some don't wanna be friends 'cause others will think they're a suck-up."

"We talked about that stuff before we decided to come here," Claire reminded. "Maybe they're not the kids you'd have as friends anyway."

"I know. And I don't want to whine about it, but it's more real now."

"All I can say is that you've gotta be you. And give it some time. Your real friends will rise to the surface. I know it's hard, but give it some time."

Joe had moved to the kitchen doorway. "She's right. You've gotta be you. Grandpa Rash always said *remember who you represent*, and I know you're always thinking of that. But also know that you shouldn't be held down by me being the principal. You gotta do what you gotta do."

Claire looked puzzled. "Are you saying he should have *punched* Sam Shottenkirk?"

"Not at all. I agree that his real friends will rise—*are rising*—to the top and that he has to be his own person and do what he feels he needs to do.

There are things that are *worth* standing up for. Sometimes that gets us in trouble, but they're still the right things. There are lots of ways to be yourself and stand up for the right things, like family. You'll handle that fine," Joe said, nodding at Elliott.

That night, Joe and Claire had a long talk about what, if anything, they could do differently to help Elliott navigate high school as the principal's kid. They could offer few ideas beyond giving it some time and encouraging Elliott to be his own person.

"I don't think we fully appreciated how you becoming principal would affect the rest of us," Claire said. "But it affects *everything.*"

Joe didn't disagree.

"But what was up with hinting that Elliott should punch that Shottenkirk kid?"

"I wasn't suggesting he do anything like that. I was just saying he has to do as he sees fit. If he gets in a fight, I'll suspend him like I would anybody else. And when I do, it will make it a whole lot harder for people to complain that some kids get special treatment around here."

"So you *want* to suspend your own kid?" Claire asked, incredulous. "Because it would benefit you?"

"Hell no. I'm just saying I'd deal with it like anything else that happens. And I was trying to lessen the burden of being the principal's kid. That's all."

Claire sighed. "Sometimes I have a hard time seeing where you're coming from. I try. I really do, but it's hard."

"I know. It's hard unless you're in it," Joe said.

QUESTIONS

1. Evaluate Joe's handling of Jodee and Alan Tursi and the mountain lion.
2. What lessons should Joe, Kristi, and Sutt take from Sutt's illness?
3. Should Joe have anticipated that tornado precautions involving senior and seventh-grade boys in the same locker room might be a problem?
4. Is Mitchell right to document Joe's failure to follow policy regarding animals in the building?
5. Appraise the way Joe responds to questions raised about Rupert Krensky by Patrazzo and Petersen.
6. What advice would you give Claire and Joe for continuing to help Elliott adjust to life as the principal's son?
7. React to Joe's statement about there being some things that are worth being suspended over. Is that an appropriate statement for a parent principal?

Chapter Eight

May

Cupcakes, Boundaries, and the Paradox

BLURRING THE LINES

Joe was immersed in commencement arrangements and individual meetings with graduating seniors when Carrie put Don Mitchell's phone call through. As usual, Mitchell blew right past any small talk. "What exactly is your wife doing with the pregnant girl?" Joe initially drew a blank before realizing Mitchell was referring to Claire's conversations with Michelle Gabus.

Mitchell said a couple school board members had raised the issue. "There is a concern that your wife is entering into the counselor's role. Or that it's being held up as a positive thing. The pregnancy, I mean."

Joe sighed, dumbfounded.

"Claire talking to the girl was the *counselor's idea*. The conversation came through an assignment in careers class about employed mothers. As I understand it, the girl doesn't have much support at home. I don't know what they talked about, but I'm sure Claire wasn't promoting the glory of teen pregnancy. I would imagine she was trying to help the girl see that she's not a horrible person and . . ."

"You don't need to be defensive. I'm just telling you the issue was raised."

"I'm sorry, Don. I don't mean to be defensive. But I don't know why they wouldn't just contact me."

"I don't know. Maybe they don't feel comfortable. Who the hell knows? But whatever the case, let's get your wife out of the counseling role, OK? Probably inappropriate."

"That's fine, Don, but my wife isn't doing any *counseling*. . . ."

"I know. Just end it."

Joe was burning. "Do you want me to tell Mrs. Barry to end the class assignment or is this just a gag order on Claire and the pregnant girl?" *You moron,* Joe thought.

"This is for your own good, Joe. Trust me. Keep your wife out of it."

"Are you gonna tell me who contacted the board members? Because unless it was Michelle Gabus's parents, I don't think it's anyone's business."

"Susan Shottenkirk. And she's certainly respected in the community and on the board. That's part of the reason I want you to get your wife out of this. Again, for your own good."

"*Of course it was Susan,*" Joe said sarcastically. "Does her status in the community give her license to judge the counselor's competence or to insert herself into another family's situation? Is there anything else Susan would like to know about the way we run this school?"

"Easy Joe, don't take it personal. You asked, I told you," Mitchell said. "You don't want to battle her. The Shottenkirks are important people in both these communities."

"I know they're important, but I'm far more concerned with *Michelle Gabus* right now, but I'll certainly talk to Susan. *Not battle* her. *Talk.* Thanks for the message, Don. Anything else?"

DID YOU EAT YOUR CUPCAKE?

Joe was happy to serve as a judge for the Advanced Technology Special Projects and was amazed at what students had designed. He was on his way out of the classroom when Den Herder grabbed his arm. "Joe, thanks for judging and for getting the Kessler tech support people down here. We really need it, especially with Altman gone."

"No problem, Coach. That's one of the benefits of the sharing arrangement. We just have to ask for the help. I'm learning those same lessons."

"Another thing, and this is important," Den Herder said, checking to see if any students were listening. "Did you eat your cupcake?"

"No, but only because I didn't know there was one."

He motioned Joe into the hallway. "I overheard some kids talking. Parker Morrissey brought them. He made them with Ex-Lax and is giving them to teachers, especially Patrazzo."

Parker's father, Jim, was a well-respected engineer at Pinicon Manufacturing and his mother worked as a nurse. Parker was a soft-spoken honor student in the senior class who had accepted a college golf scholarship. Joe knew him only casually.

"Whoa. That's good to know. Thanks."

May: Cupcakes, Boundaries, and the Paradox 123

Before heading out on his rounds through the building, he tapped out an e-mail message telling staff not to eat any cupcakes given to them and that he would be back in touch. Fifteen minutes later, Patrazzo was waiting in Joe's office. "Do you have time for me?" he asked.

"Absolutely." I came by your room but you weren't there."

Patrazzo took a seat and placed a chocolate cupcake in the center of Joe's table. "Can we talk about these?"

"Den Herder told me Parker Morrissey brought them. He overheard some kids say they have Ex-Lax in them. I'm glad you didn't eat it," Joe said.

"Right. One of my kids showed me Parker's Facebook page. He posted something about making *delicious treats from the Morrissey bakery* and that *payback's a bitch*."

"And so?" Joe asked. "What am I missing?"

"I know for a fact that this cupcake has Ex-Lax in it. A bunch of students told me not to eat it. Do you know how sick I could have gotten? I have severe allergies and could have been hospitalized! I'm pressing charges!"

"Just hang on. Is there any reason Parker would be upset with you?"

"No idea," Patrazzo shrugged.

"I'm glad you didn't eat it. Let me get him in here and see what's going on, OK? Carrie, get Parker Morrissey down here, please. And I'll get back with you, Pat. And leave the cupcake."

Parker arrived in Joe's office just seconds after Patrazzo had left.

"With graduation so close, I'm talking with every senior to see about their future plans. You must be excited about golf at Southeastern. Has it been a fast senior year for you?"

Joe grabbed a couple paper towels from the desk behind him, slid one in front of Parker and began unwrapping the cupcake. "Split it with me? Someone gave it to Mr. Patrazzo and he didn't want it, so he gave it to me and I never turn down treats," Joe said, arranging the paper towels.

"Uh, yeah, a fast year. Pretty fun. You don't want to eat that, though."

"What are you talking about? I love cupcakes, pie, ice cream, you name it."

Parker pulled the cupcake toward him. "Yours is in your mailbox," he said, gesturing toward the outer office. "This one's not OK to eat."

"Forget it. We're gonna enjoy a little treat while we talk about your golf future."

Parker hesitated, searching for words. Then he spoke. "It was for Mr. Patrazzo and has Ex-Lax in it. To get back at him for what he did to Rich Eshler," he blurted.

"Parker, what are you talking about?"

Parker explained that the cupcakes began as a make-up assignment for Barry's foods class. He had been absent for several consecutive Fridays working with a golf pro and missed a number of cooking labs. He said Barry refused to allow him to make up missed assignments and that he had made the cupcakes hoping to receive credit. "My grade has gone from an A to a C because she has labs and pop quizzes on the days I'm gone and she won't let me make them up. I've tried to do stuff in advance, but she says she never knows what we'll be doing."

"What does that have to do with Mr. Patrazzo and Rich?" Joe asked.

Parker said that a couple weeks before, Patrazzo's social problems class had been discussing controversial issues.

"And did you object to that discussion?" Joe asked.

"I like the class and *used* to like Mr. Patrazzo, but what he did to Rich was wrong," he said sharply. "The things he put on the board were way out of line. And he did it when he knew Rich was just gonna sit there and take it 'cause he couldn't say anything."

Joe was lost, but continued to dig. After several minutes of questioning, Joe had a better picture of a convoluted mess. Parker had, in fact, been absent from school attending a golf clinic on the day in question, but heard about it from classmates. They told Parker that Patrazzo had written things on the board like "Marriage is between one man and one woman," and "Guns don't kill people, bad guys do," and "Muslims represent a threat to America."

"And he does it on the *Day of Silence*? Get real," Parker said.

Joe's mind raced, remembering that Rich Eshler and a few other students had participated in the Day of Silence to call attention to support for LGBT students. Parker said Patrazzo had obviously written the statements on a day he knew Rich Eshler would not speak up.

Joe sighed. "Parker, do you know that someone could be seriously ill from taking Ex-Lax without knowing it? We're not talking a payback prank. It's *criminal*. Do you get that?"

"I didn't think about him getting, like, way sick."

"You're almost out of high school. It's time to *start thinking*. And you *weren't even there* to get the whole story! Wonder what your golf coach will think. Where are the other cupcakes?"

"In my locker."

"Bring all of them here. I don't want you to say a word about any of this to anyone until you and I talk again. Zero. Got that? And you're telling me if I eat mine or any of the others or give it to my four-year-old daughter, it's fine?"

"Yep," Parker said.

Sitting in his office, Joe did a quick experiment with a few Twitter hash tags like #PiniconDayOfSilence, #Payback, and #Cupcakes. A look at a few students' Facebook statuses, including Parker's, which was locked, yielded nothing. *That might mean no one's talking about this or that Twitter and Facebook are yesterday's news for students.* Just a couple days prior, he and

Murphy had talked about how students were migrating to other forms of social media that were harder to track.

He pulled in a few students from Patrazzo's class, who described a lively class discussion on the day in question. Rich Eshler said that he desperately wanted to participate in Patrazzo's class but had pledged not to that day. Talking to students from Barry's foods class indicated that they often had unannounced labs or quizzes on Fridays, most of which corresponded with days Parker had been absent for his sessions with the golf pro.

Following this, Joe walked to Patrazzo's room and motioned him into the hall. "Parker said he made a cupcake with Ex-Lax in it because he was upset about things you wrote on the board in social problems a couple weeks ago."

"What things? There's been a bunch of stuff on the board."

"On the Day of Silence. Something about marriage being between one man and one woman and Rich Eshler having to just sit there and take it."

Patrazzo said Rich hadn't said a word that day, which surprised him. "He's usually pretty outspoken. What's the Day of Silence, anyway?"

Joe shared what he knew of the day and asked Patrazzo to share his lesson plans, which called for students to choose a controversial statement with which they disagreed and write a short reaction essay. "It's something Watters brought back from the conference. You make kids take positions they don't like in order to get them to understand other perspectives. Kinda cool."

"Ok. I've got more to do on this. I'll be back. Thanks, Pat."

His next conversation was with Barry, who admitted adjusting the cooking lab and quiz schedule. "I was trying to send the boy a message about priorities. He needs to be here instead of playing golf every Friday. Do you know he's missed four of the last six Fridays?"

Joe said he didn't know Parker's attendance without looking and that he understood that schedules often need adjusting. "But, Joyce, you're manipulating the schedule to make a point with a single kid. You can't do that. It's not fair to him or to the rest of the students. Have you allowed him to makeup the assignments or do them in advance?"

"No. If he wants the points, he should be here, like every other student. Simple."

ACTION AND REACTION

After a quick call to McHale, Mitchell, and the state school administrators association, Joe had a little more confidence moving forward. It appeared that, if Patrazzo had eaten the cupcake and gotten sick, Parker could have been charged with administering a harmful substance and possibly a class D felony. McHale advised that he tell Barry that Parker had to be allowed to make up missed assignments, period. Armed with that knowledge and advice, Joe had called Parker's father, emphasizing the words "possible felony."

"I don't know what to say. Parker's never really been in trouble. Certainly nothing like this," he said. "What happens now?"

"I'm not sure yet. I just want you to know what's been going on," Joe said.

Joe explained the situation to Parker, who seemed remorseful and somewhat convinced that the timing of the lesson wasn't an intentional shot at Rich Eshler. "Parker, I like the fact that you wanna support a friend, but think about it. You *weren't even there* and now look at all this. I'm glad no one ate the cupcakes, but your reputation took a serious hit," Joe said. "It's a shame you're going to finish high school with this hanging over your head."

"I know I damaged my reputation, but Mrs. Barry started it. So what are you gonna do to me?"

Joe told Parker he wasn't sure yet and directed him to get his books and take a seat in the adjacent detention room. Then he left to catch Barry during her planning time.

"I'd like to know what action you're taking with Parker," she said pointedly.

"I'm not sure yet. I need some time to weigh things and think through a process."

"I see. How long does it take to *think* through something like this? It seems fairly obvious to me."

"Of course, Joyce. Parker reacted inappropriately to a well-thought lesson in Pat's class. He also reacted inappropriately to a missed lab in yours."

"Inappropriately? You mean *criminally*," she countered.

Joe ignored her comment and pushed on. "Let's keep this about you and your class here. He's got to be given the opportunity to complete things he's missed in your class." Joyce raised her finger to speak, but Joe shushed her. "I've checked the attendance records. He's been doing that with other teachers. He's got to have that opportunity with you."

Barry's face and neck flushed. "This boy can pick and choose when he comes to school because he and his family think golf is more important than school? And you're condoning that? And you come to my room to tell me *I'm* in the wrong?"

Joe lowered his voice, hoping it would calm her. "I'm telling you that there are standards for handling this. Parker is seventeen. He's gonna screw up. We're supposed to be *experts* and *professionals* who use good judgment. We can't pick and choose what kids can make up work and what kids can't, Joyce."

Barry cut him off. "So you're telling me this is my fault?" she shrieked.

"I'm telling you that Parker is to have the opportunity to complete missed work and that your class schedule should not be changed based on his presence or absence."

"I've never seen anything like this," she said, voice trembling, as she slammed an oven door hard.

"If that's not something you're willing to do, please let me know," Joe said as he left.

Joe suspended Parker at school for two days on the condition that he make a sincere apology to both teachers. He also told Patrazzo that he fully supported the intent of his lesson and noted the coincidental timing of it coming on the Day of Silence.

"I guess I should have known about that. I *am* teaching the social problems class," Patrazzo said.

"Are you comfortable with Parker's suspension?" Joe asked.

Patrazzo hesitated. "Mostly, I guess. I'm not gonna push anything. I talked to him about it and I think the point has been made. He's not a bad kid."

Barry steered clear of Joe for the remainder of the year.

THE PROM EXPERT

"I need to speak to the prom expert," Sutt said into the phone. "I've got a real mess here."

"No one here by that title, but I'll do what I can," Joe said. "How are you feeling?"

"I've been working out every day and installed that calorie counter thing on my phone. It tracks everything." He also complained that missing more than a week of work had thrown him hopelessly behind and that he found himself reacting to one crisis after another when he returned to school. "I've figured out that I will never get all of the fires put out. So I do the best I can, eat a salad, get a workout, and then get my ass home at a decent time. Oh, and Jen signed us up for a yoga class. Picture *that*!"

Sutt said the Oswald prom had gone well with no disruptions. "It's the damn post-prom party that is killing us now," he complained. "I'm not even supposed to be involved, but the other assistant principal is still out on maternity leave, so I'm covering some of her stuff."

Sutt said a volunteer mom at the post prom party had kicked out a disruptive boy whom her daughter had previously dated. An hour later, the boy's father showed up, smelling of alcohol and ready to fight.

"Ugh, another reality TV show," Joe sighed, "but if it's all parent run, how are you getting pulled in?"

"The dad of the kicked-out boy is demanding to meet with somebody and the volunteers who run post-prom are complaining that the school isn't standing behind them."

"Yuck," Kristi said. "That's tough. I'd still avoid meeting them unless Rudy makes you. It's a slippery slope."

Joe agreed. "No way. It's parent run. Not a school event. Not your jurisdiction. Once you blur that line, you'll get pulled into everything," Joe said.

"I'm with you, but Rudy says it's the classic case of how a non-school event becomes the principal's issue. They say let him come in, blow off steam, and let him spin himself out, but I hate to crack the door open to who knows what. I may let him come in and just listen," Sutt said. "I'm looking forward to getting together with you and Kristi in June, dude. We've got a lot to talk about, man."

START AT THE LOWEST LEVEL

Joe decided to address Susan Shottenkirk on her turf. Although he thought she was a full-blown phony who was not to be trusted, she and her affluent, influential family were certainly not going anywhere. As long as he stayed at Pinicon, Joe would have to work with her in some capacity. If he couldn't win her over completely, he supposed that was fine, but hoped that she wouldn't become a powerful, full-fledged adversary.

Joe knew that a fair amount of his headaches from the year had her fingerprints on them. She had complained about Kessler transfers getting special treatment, unequal sports playing time, and free physicals; complained to board members about Allison Jesup's poetry unit; spoken negatively about the sharing arrangement with Kessler in *The Pinicon Herald*; and blamed some of the ruckus at the Piedmont-Pinicon basketball game on the Kessler transfer players losing their composure. Her going directly to acting superintendent Mitchell to question Claire's casual visit with Michelle Gabus wasn't surprising, but it irritated Joe more because it involved his wife. *And don't forget her going apeshit when I suspended Sam for the Confederate flag thing*, Joe thought. *She's had a busy year making problems for me.*

Joe's conversations with Karl Ortiz at the Trailways and Micah Krensky at Krensky Auto had been fairly successful. He thought the same tactic might work with Susan. Perhaps she would see it as a peace offering, that he wasn't intimidated, or both. Joe thought about calling ahead to make an appointment, but decided against it because he didn't want to give Susan the opportunity to prepare. *Plus, people jump me with no notice all the time at school, at the game, grocery store, or in the front yard. Why not try the same ap-*

proach? He found Susan working on her computer in her well-appointed office at Shottenkirk Tire and Appliance.

"Hi Susan. Do you have a minute?" She looked up, clearly surprised to see him. "Absolutely, Mr. Gentry. Can I get you a cup of coffee or something? Come on in. How can I help you today?"

She has the sappy sweet rap down, Joe thought, remembering how Young said she was skilled at stabbing people in the back while giving them a hug.

"I wanted to touch base with you on the concern you raised with a couple of board members."

"Oh. And what concern was that?"

Joe laughed. "Well, I only know about one. I don't know how often you've been in contact with them," he said, trying to sound nonchalant, wondering if she was playing dumb or whether she had actually raised so many issues that she couldn't keep track of them. *It's possible*, he thought.

Joe referenced Claire talking with Michelle Gabus. Susan said her main concern was that the girl was getting the professional help she needed and wasn't being passed off. "It must be *so hard* for Michelle, with her family situation and all."

Her condescending tone made Joe's skin crawl. "Kids do have a lot to deal with nowadays, no matter who they are. We spend a lot of time working on making our school a comfortable and supportive place for every kid, regardless of their unique situation."

Susan nodded sweetly.

"Part of that is being receptive to parent concerns. You and I have had some differences of opinion and we may again in the future. I hope you'll share your perspective with *me and the teachers directly*. We want to address things as close to the source as possible, just like a customer who comes directly to you rather than going straight to Goodyear headquarters for a problem with their tires."

Susan seemed uncomfortable. "I hope the school staff has the expertise to work with girls like Michelle and that we're not pushing kids off to others," she said. "I guess I want the board members to know what tough jobs all of you at the school have. I sure couldn't do it," she said sweetly.

Bullshit, Joe thought. *She doesn't want the board to know about our tough jobs. She wants to make us look bad.* Joe said he appreciated her concern for Pinicon kids and restated his open-door policy for talking about them directly. "I know you're busy and I'll let you get back to work. I just wanted to stop by and extend the invitation."

He wanted to address Susan's meddling with board members, but also wanted to defend Jeralyn's idea for Claire to talk with Michelle Gabus. And he wanted to send the message that Susan could dislike him as much as she wanted but to leave his wife out of it. He hoped that his approach would accomplish multiple goals, but without getting into any specifics or justifying things. McHale said it was worth a shot. Time would tell.

BOUNDARIES AND RIPPLES

Joe was surprised and disappointed that Pinicon Floral and Gifts had refused to sell or deliver flowers to Rich Eshler. Like all of the Pinicon main street businesses, the store enjoyed a solid relationship with the school. Joe and the leadership team had worked hard to make sure the relationship felt like a true partnership. "We can't have it appear like we're just asking for donations all the time. We have to try and give the businesses our support whenever we can, whether it's allowing students to earn credit by working in the careers program or just buying things in Pinicon," he had written in his blog. He was surprised that store owner Betty Wardenberg, a pleasant grandmotherly figure and former school board member, had refused to deliver flowers to Rich Eshler.

On Saturday morning Joe and Margaret stopped in to buy some flowers for Claire. If the time seemed right, he planned to mention his disappointment over the Rich Eshler decision. Betty was as pleasant as ever as Margaret examined the cooler full of fresh flowers. After a little small talk about the weather, Betty provided the opening Joe wanted by making a reference to how nice all the kids looked at the prom. "It's always nice to see them all dressed up," she said.

"It sure is. And just about everything went off without a hitch, including the weather," Joe said.

"Oh? What didn't go smoothly?"

"The school parts of it went perfectly. The kids couldn't have been better. I was a little surprised when I heard that your store wouldn't deliver to Rich Eshler."

Betty looked up from her worktable. "We had so many orders it was hard to get them all ready on time. And the order for the Eshler boy came in *after the deadline*. The kids know orders have to be placed by the Wednesday before prom; otherwise, we won't have enough flowers."

"I see. I wonder if Rich's date, a Hillcrest student, knew that."

"You mean the *boy* he brought to the prom. The truth is, even if the order had come in on time, which it didn't, we wouldn't have delivered it. I don't know why they want to make a mockery of everything."

"*They?*" Joe asked.

"Those kids."

"Which kids are those?"

Betty wasn't going to take the bait. Instead she said, "Mr. Gentry, we've run our business the way we see fit for twenty-four years and will continue."

"Absolutely," Joe said. "I was just surprised and disappointed. I hate to see unnecessary things hurt kids and set some apart."

Betty paused. "That's not really my concern. There are other flower shops."

"Absolutely. There are lots of places for folks to buy flowers. Or for the school to buy them, for that matter," Joe said, referencing the school's purchase of flowers for the National Honor Society induction ceremony, graduation, and a handful of other events. "But we buy them *here*."

Betty's expression tightened.

Margaret was growing impatient. "The yellow ones, dad. Let's get the yellow ones," she said, pointing to a bouquet of daffodils.

Betty slid open the door and retrieved them. "They're beautiful, aren't they, sweetie?" she asked, wrapping and handing them to Margaret.

It was as if only Margaret and Betty were in the shop now. She rang up the purchase pleasantly, prattling on with Margaret, barely acknowledging Joe's presence. "Thanks so much for coming in. I hope mom enjoys the flowers, sweetie." Joe thanked Betty, wished her a good weekend, and headed out into the morning sun with Margaret.

CELEBRATE SUCCESS

Joe had just finished establishing a second Twitter account under the name "PirateGuy99." Even though he and Cal Murphy at Kessler had noted that many students were migrating to other forms of social media, he wondered if a generic, anonymous Twitter profile would allow him to gain information that he might not find through other channels. He briefly wondered if setting up a bogus account for that purpose was entirely ethical, but convinced himself that it was just another way to be situationally aware, as Professor Summers had preached. *The ends justify the means. Wait till I tell Sutt*, he mused, wondering if other principals had similar accounts.

After selecting a pirate picture for PirateGuy99's profile picture, several members of the leadership team walked in. Martinson and Watters carried cupcakes and a jug of lemonade. Richards, Prior, Den Herder, and Young stood behind. "We thought a small celebration is in order," Watters said.

"I'm a little leery of cupcakes, folks," Joe said, leaning on his desk. "But I like celebrations. Tell me what we're celebrating."

"We just met to talk about those kids you asked us to try and connect with. We looked at the list and their attendance and grades compared to the end of the fall semester and this time last year. And the news is pretty decent. Several of them are in a little better shape. Robin Stiles is steady. Oliver Ortiz has been staying all day, and Rupert Krensky is working on a model citizen award," Watters said.

"That's a little strong, but they *are* turning in *work*," Den Herder said. "Plus the cupcakes were two for one."

"And it's possible they're a day old," Young added.

"Kidding aside, there are some tough kids who are hanging in there. We know it is a collective effort, but a lot of that starts at the top. It would have been easy to deal with other stuff, but you've helped us move them forward. These were kids falling through the cracks and Pinicon ought to be the kind of school where that doesn't happen," Watters said.

"Part of the Pinicon Way of working with kids," Martinson said, giggling a little.

Joe smiled. "Treats and breaks have a way of coming right when you need them, don't they? But it's not me. If anything good has happened, it's because of a team effort. Really thoughtful of you all. Thanks. One last time, who baked these?"

The group broke out laughing.

WHO'S MEDDLING?

Joe was enjoying a beer and watching the charcoal burn when Claire stepped on to the patio. "When you and Margaret bought those daffodils did you talk to Betty Wardenberg?"

Joe paused. "Yeah. Small talk mostly, but I also told her I was disappointed they said they wouldn't deliver flowers to Rich Eshler. She's a nice lady but she's also a bigot."

"Did you argue with her?"

"No, but I told her I was disappointed they did that to a kid. She said she would run their business the way they see fit and people can get flowers whereever they want."

"Did you tell her the school was no longer going to do business with her shop?"

Joe cocked his head. "No. She said people could get flowers anywhere. I told her she was right but that we choose to get them there because it's the *right thing to do*. Why?"

"You know our store was doing a remodel of her shop. All new fixtures, flooring, lighting, display cases, the works. Betty called today to say they're giving the job to someone else. Looks like she's getting back at both of us by taking her business to our main competitor." Claire had been working on the design and fixtures for weeks, and the job was expected to be in the $15,000–20,000 range.

"Those few hundred bucks the school spends a year just cost me and the store twenty grand! Just the other day you were mad at Susan Shottenkirk for meddling with the board on the Michelle Gabus deal. *Who's meddling now?*"

"Claire, I wasn't meddling. I was *sticking up* for a Pinicon kid who was being mistreated and singled out. I didn't say we weren't buying stuff from her."

"I know you want to defend the kid and I respect that, but it's not how she took it. She thinks you threatened to pull the school's business. You looked like a dictator, lost credibility, and my store lost a $20,000 job," Claire said, turning to go back into the house.

SKYPE CONFERENCE

Joe shared the apparent push-back from Betty at Pinicon Floral and Gifts and how his visit there had apparently cost Walsh Furniture and Design a bundle. "I've felt sick about it. I apologized to Claire's boss, who didn't have much to say. If Don Mitchell finds out, I'm sure he'll blow a gasket. I look like a real loser in this deal."

Sutt and Kristi disagreed. "You called them out for the way they treated one of your kids. I don't see anything wrong with that," Kristi said. "The owner wanted to be petty. That's on her." Sutt predicted that over the long haul, Joe would feel better about it, but acknowledged that it put Claire in an awkward position. "Sometimes the politics suck, but they never go away."

Kristi countered that it was a good move for Joe to let her know where he stood in his first year on the job. They ended their conversation by comparing who had the most paperwork and teacher evaluations to finish by the end of the year and promised to exchange plans for their final faculty meetings, before Kristi started throwing out dates for their gathering back at the Northgate Grill in June.

SUNDAY REFLECTION

Professor Summers, Murphy, and the other conference principals had told Joe the end of the school year would come in a crush. With spring in full bloom, he badly wanted to be somewhere other than his office on Sunday afternoon, but he told Claire he needed a couple of hours to catch up. Many of the items on his end-of-the-year checklist reminded him of experiences gained, lessons learned, and things yet left undone.

The committee of ADs established by the conference principals to examine sportsmanship had yielded essentially nothing. There were no more reports of racially charged fan behavior after Joe had drawn the group's attention to events at the Piedmont-Pinicon basketball game. He wasn't surprised, though. *Not a lot of crazy fans at spring track meets*, he said to himself. *Having set the stage, I'll pounce if this comes up again next year.*

On a more positive note, student and faculty efforts to nail down the Pinicon Way left him encouraged. Though differently stated, teachers' and students' definitions shared many similarities, including a supportive, student-centered environment; active engagement in athletics, the arts, and academics; an emphasis on group problem solving; and continuous growth, creativity, and high expectations.

He hired a graphic artist to produce posters featuring both versions and the Pinicon Pirate logo, and planned to display them everywhere in the fall. He tried to contract with Richards to make plaques for installation outside each teacher and staff member's workspace displaying their picture, college alma mater, and the faculty statement of the Pinicon Way. Richards agreed, but would accept no payment, instead suggesting the money go to the Pinicon Scholarship Fund. He smiled as he looked at Crawford's plaque, knowing the support staff would be surprised to get them too. *I can't wait to get these hung up and do a better job of tying everything we do to this.*

Other projects reminded him of how much of school leadership is ongoing. Small groups of teachers had begun examining student test scores and content, as he had pitched in February. While some teachers dug into the topic aggressively, he wondered if there were simply too many other things underway to do the process justice. *I might have started that one too late. Or let the Pinicon Way stuff take too long.*

Other things nagged at him. He had wondered several times if he should have tried to do something with the Middle Eastern school featured in Pinicon's opening ceremony. *Some kind of partnership makes sense, but maybe the timing was all wrong. Or maybe it was a missed opportunity.* Likewise, several teachers, their instruction, and Joe's relationship with them seemed to be in a holding pattern. *I need some serious time to think about next steps.*

Then there was Mitchell. Joe remembered being nervous for his midyear evaluation, which turned out to be pretty benign. But that was before Joe had allowed the mountain lion into school, met Karl Ortiz at the Trailways, had Claire talking with Michelle Gabus, and handled a few other issues in ways that apparently stirred Mitchell's ire.

He was also unsure of what, if anything, to do with his impression that Mitchell may have manipulated the process by which some former Kessler students wound up at Pinicon. It seemed that some problem students, like Mace Stallworth and Rupert Krensky, were simply sent to Pinicon, while others like Javaris Hayes had to negotiate a strange process. Joe had vowed to ask about it, but with no idea when or if Zylstra would return as superintendent, he wondered if it would be better to keep his head down, especially with Mitchell wanting to meet in early June for his formal evaluation. Looking back over the year, he was exhausted, but in a good kind of way. His frustrations, misjudgments, and mistakes burned and irritated him, while signs of progress and success were sources of energy and optimism.

And finally, there was the question of balance—between leadership and management, personal and professional, pushing and pulling, equality and fairness, enough and too much. At times, he felt certain that he had improved in all of these areas. At other times, it seemed things could turn on a dime, throwing an elusive balance woefully out of whack. *Maybe it's always like that*, he thought.

His phone buzzed with a text from Claire: *Time 2 come home. Bike ride.*

OUT THE DOOR

Joe wondered if there was a way to anticipate how the student body would handle the end of the school year. Horror stories from Murphy and other principals describing end-of-the-year tragedies like rowdy parties, car accidents, and suicides had him on edge. Though he learned of it late, he enthusiastically granted the student council's request to participate in the Smart Decisions program, which, among other things, placed a wrecked car on the front lawn of the school to remind students of the dangers of drinking and driving. Next year, Joe hoped to join other conference schools in starting the program earlier, closer to prom, sending student leaders to a two-day retreat, and inviting the group to conduct an assembly at Pinicon.

In individual meetings with seniors, several had hinted at a senior skip day. As a result, Joe met with three different groups of seniors, including Sam Shottenkirk and Bryce Cone, who appeared to be leading the idea. He reinforced the same message in a senior class meeting. "You seniors already get out several days early. You'd have to make up the missed time and wouldn't walk across the stage at graduation if everything's not taken care of. Don't screw up a great year right at the end."

He was optimistic that skip day was just talk, but on the Thursday before the seniors' last day, 42 were notably absent. More than a little irritated, Joe found the location on his PirateGuy99 Twitter feed and sped out to the state park in Young's Camaro, apprehensive about what awaited him.

Despite his initial ire, he found it hard to be angry. The seniors were playing bean bags and tossing the football around while smoke billowed from grills filled with hamburgers and hot dogs. An intuitive park ranger had just completed taking down all their names on a legal pad when Joe drove up. "We get one of these skip days out here every few years. What a bunch of nice kids. No booze or anything, I already checked," the ranger said, handing Joe the list of names. *I need to send this guy a Pinicon t-shirt*, Joe thought.

Joe declined their offer for a hot dog and reminded them as firmly as he could that they would have to make up the time and that the clock was running. "Anyone who has time left to make up won't be participating in the graduation ceremony."

He drove back to school, much slower than on his way to the park, laughing to himself. Despite the time and effort he had spent warning students not to skip, they did anyway. He knew he was in for many more hours sorting through bogus excuses that were surely coming from some parents.

Yet, he was not particularly angry or upset. Part of it was because the kids weren't rowdy, destructive, or breaking the law. *Their cookout was about as tame is it could get*, he smiled. He had done his due diligence in warning them against skipping, and they did anyway. He would move forward according to policy, just as he had explained he would. *No big deal.*

He took the long way back to school, driving alongside the Pinicon River as he savored the warm, spring sun, the calm scene at the park, and Young's meticulously restored Camaro. As the car purred along the blacktop, he thought back to Professor Summers's final grad school lecture. He could see Summers pacing the room in his blue Brooks Brothers suit discussing the Paradox of the Principalship.

Summers argued that the principalship is a paradox of seemingly competing functions that have to be navigated, tamed, and balanced. "Every school in the country wants *leadership*, but you'll get fired if you can't handle *management*. While leadership and management are in some ways distinct, the great ones realize the way they manage reveals a lot about their leadership. Leadership and management should actually be *in synergy*, not opposition. The great ones also say difficult things that people don't want to hear, but with care and in a way that doesn't alienate them. I call it being *tactfully blunt*."

Speaking on the principal's duties, Summers said, "We must be passionately *committed* to doing the right things, not just easy or noncontroversial things. At the same time, we have to know that, despite our best efforts, we'll fall short sometimes. We have to *detach* from those failures and rise to fight for the right things again, still with passion and commitment. The great ones balance passion, commitment, and detachment, all at the same time."

The final component of Summers's paradox addressed the gamut of principals' responsibilities. "The hours are exhausting and the issues are endless, but just when we feel we can't handle one more thing, something will remind us of the privilege of being *difference makers*. Embrace that and trust that those moments are present, even when we can't see them because we're in the center of the storm."

It felt as though through all the ups and downs of his first year as principal, the stars had aligned on senior skip day to provide Joe some new insight and clarity. He didn't think he had mastered the job or even Summers's Paradox of the Principalship. He knew he'd made plenty of mistakes during his first year. But that day, he felt he *understood* the job and what Summers meant by the paradox in a way that he had not before. *Maybe it's the end of the year and prospect for taking a break*, he thought. *Maybe it's a smooth stretch of highway, a classic car, a warm day, and no death and destruction at the state park.* Whatever the case, Joe felt like he could drive forever, thinking.

Over the next few days, flimsy excuses from parents, some of whom were school board members, teachers, and community big shots, rolled in. Explanations ranged from the generic *needed at home*, to visiting sick relatives, to getting measured for a tuxedo for a summer wedding. All told, Joe figured he spent about twenty hours sorting it all. He tried to apply the lessons of the paradox throughout the process. All of the offending seniors made up the time Joe required of them, but only after he reduced the time for several, based on excuses from their parents that he knew were a joke but could never prove. Professor Summers's advice to "control what you can control" and "to see some of this craziness as just good entertainment" rang in his head. *Summers is right. Sometimes the best you can do is to send a message*, he reflected.

Other than skip day, a handful of other pranks, and poorly timed field trips for underclassmen, the end of the year was smooth. Graduation weekend brought weather that was again perfect. Joe joined Dave Crawford and a handful of students on the final session of Saturday School to wash windows and to triple check the sound system, number of chairs, programs, and details of the ceremony. On McHale's advice, he had met privately with the students scheduled to speak and reviewed the text of their speeches. He was secretly happy that Don Mitchell would not be attending the Pinicon ceremony because Kessler's graduation was scheduled for the same time.

Joe's remarks were brief and to the point, knowing that no one wants a long graduation ceremony. In the same blue-and-gold tie he had worn on the first day of school, he thanked parents, faculty, staff, and students for a memorable year and reminded them to "hold tightly to the pride that makes Pinicon such a special place." Then he pulled his grandfather's buckeye from his pocket and revisited the story he had shared with the staff ten months earlier.

"Graduating seniors, I wish you luck and challenge you to live well, work hard, laugh often, love much, and remember the foundation you have laid here at Pinicon. Your future begins at the north doors of the gym. Congratulations."

On a small table just off the stage, Joe had placed a bowl of buckeyes, one for each graduate.

QUESTIONS

1. Evaluate the way Joe responded to Don Mitchell's questions about Claire talking to Michelle Gabus.

2. Did Joe respond effectively to the cupcake incident? Would you have acted differently?
3. Assess Joe's meeting with Susan Shottenkirk.
4. Evaluate Joe's interaction with Betty Wardenberg at the flower shop. Did Joe overstep or act appropriately?
5. Joe, Sutt, and Kristi agree to share their plans for the final faculty meeting. What should Joe include?
6. React to Joe's reflections and questions on his way back to school from senior skip day and to Professor Summers's Paradox of the Principalship.

FINAL QUESTIONS

1. As they did during winter break, Joe, Sutt, and Kristi plan to meet in June to reflect on their first year as principals. What would you expect to hear in terms of lessons learned? Do you feel Joe applied lessons learned from formal and informal mentors? What predictions do you have for their second and subsequent years as school leaders?
2. Using the appropriate school leadership standards for your state and/or district, conduct a thorough, year-end evaluation of Joe's first year as principal. Organize your evaluation in the format used by your state/district.

   - Develop a plan for how you would conduct the meeting with Joe to share the evaluation.
   - Cite evidence that can be aligned with specific criteria and note particular strengths and improvement areas.
   - Which standards do you see as strengths for Joe to build upon? Which standards do you see as improvement areas?

References

Fiore, D. J., & Whitaker, T. (2005). *Six types of teachers: Recruiting, retaining and mentoring the best.* Larchmont, NY: Eye on Education.
Haley, A. (2007). *Roots: The saga of an American family.* Cambridge, MA: Vanguard Books.
Haley, A. (1966). The *Playboy* interview: George Lincoln Rockwell. *Playboy,* 13(4), 71–72, 74, 76–82, 154, 156.
Hemmingway, E. (2012). *A farewell to arms.* New York, NY: Scribner.
Lencioni, P. M. (2002). *The five dysfunctions of a team: A leadership fable.* San Francisco, CA: Jossey-Bass.
Loewen, J. W. (2007). *Lies my teacher told me: Everything your American History textbook got wrong.* New York, NY: Simon & Schuster.
O' Brien, T. (1990). *The things they carried.* New York, NY: Houghton Mifflin Harcourt.
Pace, N. J. (2013). *Reality calling: The story of a principal's first semester.* Lanham, MD: Rowman & Littlefield Education.
Peale, N. V. (2003). *The power of positive thinking.* New York, NY: Simon & Schuster.
Tatum, B. D. (1997). *Why are all the Black kids sitting together in the cafeteria?* New York, NY: Basic Books.
X, Malcolm, & Haley, A. (1999). *The autobiography of Malcolm X.* New York, NY: Ballantine Publishing Group.

www.ingramcontent.com/pod-product-compliance
Lightning Source LLC
Chambersburg PA
CBHW030115010526
44116CB00005B/260